The CompTIA Network+ & Security+ Certification: 2 in 1 Book- Simplified Study Guide
Eighth Edition (Exam N10-008)
Ace5

This book is published by BC Seminary Publishers.

Paperback Edition

First Edition: 2023

ISBN: **978-1-961902-33-6**

Printed in the USA.

In God We Trust

N:B: 50% Proceed from These Sales will Be Used to Support the Less Privileged in Africa and the Middle East.

Table of Contents

Introduction

In a world dominated by technology and interconnectedness, networks have become the lifeblood of organizations and daily activities. A profound understanding of network principles, protocols, and operations is imperative for anyone aspiring to thrive in the Information Technology (IT) field. The CompTIA Network+ certification is a globally esteemed credential that authenticates an individual's proficiency in networking. Whether you are embarking on your IT journey or an experienced professional keen on broadening your knowledge and qualifications, this exhaustive guide is engineered to be the definitive resource for mastering the CompTIA Network+ exam.

CompTIA, the Computing Technology Industry Association, is a non-profit trade association that provides professional certifications for the IT industry. It is one of the most recognized and respected associations in the IT world, offering a range of certifications from entry-level to expert level. The Network+ certification is a mid-level certification designed for network technicians and is often a stepping stone to more advanced certifications like the CompTIA Security+ or vendor-specific certifications like Cisco's CCNA.

The significance of the Network+ certification extends beyond just another accolade on your resume. It serves as an endorsement of your capabilities to design, configure, manage, and troubleshoot networks, thereby validating your expertise to both current and potential employers. The exam encompasses a broad spectrum of topics, from foundational networking concepts such as the OSI and TCP/IP models, IP addressing, and subnets, to intricate subjects like network security, disaster recovery, and industry standards and compliance requirements.

This guide is meticulously crafted to offer a comprehensive understanding of all facets covered by the CompTIA Network+ exam. Chapter 1 initiates with the fundamental Networking Concepts, encompassing network topologies, networking devices, ports, and protocols. Progressing to chapter 2, you will be acquainted with the intricacies of network installation and configuration, including LAN/WAN technologies, wireless networks, and DHCP and DNS configuration. Chapter 3 delves deeper into network media and topologies, elaborating on cable types, connectors, network architecture, and VLANs.

Maintaining the seamless operation of a network is a pivotal responsibility for any network professional. Chapter 4 concentrates on network operations, encompassing network monitoring, configuration management, and disaster recovery. Chapter 5 is devoted to network security, a critical dimension of networking that includes firewalls, IDS/IPS systems, VPNs, and adherence to security policies. Troubleshooting is an unavoidable aspect of a network professional's role, and chapter 6 covers the methodologies, tools, and common challenges encountered in network troubleshooting.

Moreover, this guide transcends the technical dimensions of the CompTIA Network+ exam. Chapter 7 explores the softer aspects of networking, elucidating industry standards, best practices, and compliance requirements that every network professional must be cognizant of. Finally, chapter 8 furnishes invaluable exam preparation tips, practice exams, answers, and exam day strategies to ensure your triumph.

This guide is structured to provide a progressive learning journey. It is recommended to start from chapter 1 and work your way through to chapter 8. Each section builds upon the previous one, ensuring a comprehensive understanding of all aspects of networking. Practice exams are included to test your knowledge and prepare you for the actual exam. Use this guide as a reference, a study tool, and a roadmap to success.

In conclusion, this exhaustive guide aspires to equip you with everything necessary to excel in the CompTIA Network+ exam. It is not merely about passing the exam but about thoroughly comprehending and mastering the concepts, skills, and practices fundamental to networking. Armed with this guide, you are poised to become a CompTIA Network+ certified professional, an achievement that will unlock opportunities and propel your career in the IT industry.

Chapter 1: CompTIA Network+

As you embark on your journey into the expansive field of Information Technology, you'll encounter a plethora of certifications that promise to enhance your skills, bolster your resume, and offer you a competitive edge in the job market. Among these myriad options, the CompTIA Network+ Certification stands out as a cornerstone credential. It's much more than a fancy acronym or a certificate to hang on your wall; it's a recognition of your expertise in networking, conferred by one of the most respected organizations in the tech industry—CompTIA.

Now, let's unpack the essence of CompTIA. The Computing Technology Industry Association, or CompTIA, is a global non-profit organization established with the mission to advance the IT industry. For decades, CompTIA has been at the forefront of setting industry standards, offering educational programs, and most importantly, administering professional certifications. The Network+ certification is just one among several credentials offered by CompTIA, but it occupies a critical space. Specifically designed for IT network practitioners, this certification is often considered the golden standard for validating the core skills needed to design, configure, manage, and troubleshoot wired and wireless networks.

The first question that likely comes to mind is, "Why Network+?" Unlike other certifications that may require years of experience or pre-existing credentials, CompTIA Network+ is accessible. It doesn't demand extensive prerequisites, making it an ideal starting point for newcomers as well as a solid stepping stone for seasoned IT professionals looking to validate their networking skills. Yet, don't let its accessibility fool you. The breadth and depth of knowledge it covers are both rigorous and comprehensive. This certification explores a wide array of topics: from networking concepts and infrastructure to network operations, security, and troubleshooting. Simply put, earning the Network+ badge is akin to obtaining a seal of approval that attests to your broad-based proficiency and understanding of current networking technologies.

Now, how does this certification stand out in a crowded marketplace of IT credentials? The CompTIA Network+ Certification is not vendor-specific. This means that the knowledge you gain is not tied to a particular brand or line of products. Instead, it equips you with universal skills and knowledge that are transferrable across a myriad of networking environments—be it Cisco, Juniper, or any other platform. This universality gives you the flexibility to maneuver through different roles in the IT landscape, from network administration to network engineering and even cybersecurity roles that demand a solid foundation in networking.

Let's turn our attention to the critical components of the exam itself. The Network+ exam is usually a single test, comprising multiple-choice, drag-and-drop, and performance-based questions that assess your theoretical knowledge as well as practical skills. The topics range from the design and implementation of functional networks and network troubleshooting to the management of essential network devices and implementation of network security protocols. Though the exam is challenging, it's fair, designed to rigorously test your understanding of networking to ensure that once you're certified, you're genuinely equipped to handle real-world networking challenges.

At this point, you might wonder what your next steps should be. Your decision to seek the CompTIA Network+ Certification is not merely a commitment to passing an exam but a strategic move towards mastering an essential domain within the IT industry. You're opening doors to enhanced career prospects, higher earning potential, and above all, a deeper, more nuanced understanding of the complex world of networking. This guide aims to be your compass, navigating you through each topic, each challenge, ensuring that when you walk into that exam room, you'll walk out as a CompTIA Network+ certified professional.

So, as you flip through the subsequent pages of this guide, know that each chapter is tailored to prepare you comprehensively for the CompTIA Network+ exam. This isn't just about learning to pass a test; it's about equipping yourself with the skills and knowledge to excel in your career for years to come.

Networking Concepts

The foundation of a successful career in IT networking lies in a solid understanding of its fundamental concepts. These concepts form the backbone of the CompTIA

Network+ certification exam and are critical to your ability to design, implement, and manage networks in a real-world environment. In this chapter, we will explore the essential networking concepts that every IT professional must know.

Introduction to Networking

Networking is the practice of connecting computers, servers, and other devices together to share resources. This could include sharing files, applications, or access to the internet. Networks can vary in size from a small local area network (LAN) in a home or office, to a wide area network (WAN) that connects devices across cities, states, or even countries.

- Types of Networks: There are several different types of networks, including LANs, WANs, and metropolitan area networks (MANs). LANs are usually confined to a small geographic area, such as a single building or campus. WANs, on the other hand, cover a larger geographic area and are typically used to connect multiple LANs. MANs fall in between, covering a larger area than a LAN but smaller than a WAN, typically a city or a large campus.

- Network Components: A network is composed of various components, each serving a specific function. These include:

    - Network Interface Cards (NICs): These are hardware components that connect a computer to a network.

    - Switches: These are devices that connect multiple computers within a LAN and use MAC addresses to forward data to the correct destination.

    - Routers: These are devices that connect different networks and use IP addresses to forward data between them.

    - Access Points: These are devices that allow wireless devices to connect to a wired network using Wi-Fi.

Understanding these basic components and how they interact is fundamental to grasping more complex networking concepts.

OSI and TCP/IP Models

To understand how data travels from one device to another over a network, it is essential to understand the OSI and TCP/IP models. These models break down the networking process into layers, with each layer having a specific function.

- OSI Model: The Open Systems Interconnection (OSI) model is a conceptual framework used to understand network interactions in seven layers. From the lowest to the highest, these layers are:

    1. Physical Layer: This layer deals with the physical connection between devices, such as cables and switches.

    2. Data Link Layer: This layer is responsible for creating a reliable link between two directly connected nodes.

    3. Network Layer: This layer is responsible for determining the best path for data to travel from the source to the destination.

    4. Transport Layer: This layer is responsible for end-to-end communication and error recovery.

    5. Session Layer: This layer manages sessions or connections between applications.

    6. Presentation Layer: This layer is responsible for data format translation, encryption, and compression.

    7. Application Layer: This layer provides the interface for applications to access network services.

- TCP/IP Model: The Transmission Control Protocol/Internet Protocol (TCP/IP) model is another conceptual framework used to understand network interactions. It is the model used by the internet and has four layers:

    1. Application Layer: This layer provides the interface for applications to access network services.

    2. Transport Layer: This layer is responsible for end-to-end communication and error recovery.

3. Internet Layer: This layer is responsible for determining the best path for data to travel from the source to the destination.

4. Link Layer: This layer deals with the physical and data link aspects of network communication.

IP Addressing and Subnets

IP addressing is a critical aspect of networking, as it allows devices to locate and communicate with each other across a network. An IP address is a unique identifier assigned to each device on a network.

- IPv4 vs. IPv6: There are two versions of IP addresses in use today: IPv4 and IPv6. IPv4 addresses are 32-bit addresses written in decimal format, for example, 192.168.1.1. IPv6 addresses are 128-bit addresses written in hexadecimal format, for example, 2001:0db8:85a3:0000:0000:8a2e:0370:7334. IPv6 was developed to address the shortage of available IPv4 addresses.

- Subnetting: Subnetting is the process of dividing an IP network into sub-networks, each having its own network address. This is done to improve performance, security, and efficiency. Understanding how to subnet is essential for any network professional.

Ports and Protocols

Ports and protocols are fundamental concepts in networking that allow devices to communicate over a network. A protocol is a set of rules that define how data is transmitted over a network. A port is a virtual endpoint for communication.

- Common Protocols: There are many protocols used in networking, each serving a specific purpose. Some common ones include:

  - HTTP (HyperText Transfer Protocol): Used for transferring web pages.

  - FTP (File Transfer Protocol): Used for transferring files.

  - SMTP (Simple Mail Transfer Protocol): Used for sending email.

  - DNS (Domain Name System): Used for resolving domain names to IP addresses.

- Ports: Ports are used to differentiate different services or applications on a single device. For example, HTTP traffic typically uses port 80, while FTP traffic typically uses port 21.

Network Topologies

A network topology is the arrangement of nodes (computers, servers, networking devices) in a network. Understanding network topologies is essential for designing and implementing networks.

Common Topologies: There are several common network topologies, including:

- Bus Topology: In a bus topology, all nodes are connected to a single communication line known as a bus.

- Star Topology: In a star topology, all nodes are connected to a central device, such as a switch or a hub.

- Ring Topology: In a ring topology, each node is connected to exactly two other nodes, forming a ring.

- Mesh Topology: In a mesh topology, nodes are interconnected, with each node connected to multiple other nodes.

Networking Devices

Understanding the function and capabilities of different networking devices is crucial for anyone working in networking. We've already touched on some essential devices like switches and routers. Let's elaborate a bit more.

- Switch: A switch is a network device that connects multiple devices within a LAN. Unlike a hub, which broadcasts data packets to all devices on a network, a switch uses MAC addresses to send data only to the intended recipient.

- Router: A router connects different networks and uses IP addresses to forward data between them. It serves as the gateway between a LAN and external networks such as the internet.

- Firewall: A firewall is a network device designed to block unauthorized access to or from a network. It can be hardware, software, or both and is essential for network security.

Each of these devices plays a unique role in a network, and understanding their functions is crucial for passing the CompTIA Network+ exam as well as for effective network management.

This chapter has provided an extensive overview of the networking concepts that form the foundation of the CompTIA Network+ exam. From understanding what networking is and its various components to diving deep into IP addressing, ports, and protocols, these are the essentials you need to grasp. As you move forward, these foundational elements will serve as the building blocks for mastering more complex subjects in networking, arming you with the skills and knowledge you need to become a certified network professional.

Chapter 2: Network Installation and Configuration

The ability to install and configure networks isn't just a skill; it's a necessity. As someone preparing for the CompTIA Network+ exam, you're looking to not only pass an exam but also to gain a well-rounded competency in setting up and configuring different types of networks. So let's delve into this crucial arena.

Firstly, let's look at the anatomy of a network. Every network, regardless of its size or purpose, requires a foundational physical setup. This is the underlying layer of hardware that makes all the data communication possible. We're talking about cables, routers, switches, and other networking devices. Each device has a role to play, whether it's routing data packets between different networks or merely connecting computers in a local area network (LAN). In larger setups, you might also encounter WAN (Wide Area Network) technologies that connect networks across geographical distances. Knowing the roles of these devices and how they work together is fundamental to setting up any network efficiently.

But what about wireless networks? In today's world, where mobility and convenience are king, wireless networks have become ubiquitous. Understanding the principles of radio frequencies, channels, and how to secure these types of networks is crucial. Wireless networks are often layered on top of existing wired networks, requiring a different set of configurations like setting up access points and determining the range and strength of your wireless signals. It's a blend of the physical and the logical, making it a compelling subject matter that demands your full attention.

As you can imagine, configuring these devices involves more than just plugging them in. That brings us to the software side of things—how to set up network services like DHCP and DNS. DHCP, or Dynamic Host Configuration Protocol, automates the IP address assignment, an otherwise manual task that could be quite labor-intensive. DNS, or Domain Name System, translates human-friendly domain names to IP addresses. Without these services, networks would be far less dynamic and much more difficult to manage. Mastering these configurations will not only make your life easier but also make you invaluable in any networking environment.

Of course, modern networks don't just exist in physical hardware; they also extend into the virtual realm. Virtualization and cloud computing are transforming the way networks are built and managed. Now you can create virtual networks, configure virtual machines, and even move your entire infrastructure to the cloud. Learning the ins and outs of virtualization techniques, as well as how to navigate and configure cloud-based resources, is increasingly becoming a must-have skill. It's also worth noting that virtualization can offer both cost savings and increases in efficiency, but only if configured correctly.

Moving on, no network exists in isolation. Therefore, understanding how to integrate your local network into larger networks via WAN technologies and the Internet is essential. This is where concepts like VPN (Virtual Private Network) come in handy. A VPN allows a secure connection over the internet, letting you interact with remote networks as if you were physically present. This includes complex configurations and security protocols that ensure data integrity and confidentiality.

Lastly, you can't talk about network installation and configuration without mentioning best practices. Networking has its share of protocols and policies, and you'll need to be well-versed in these to maintain a secure, efficient environment. This is not just about the technical details but also about the governance policies like compliance with industry standards and regulations. A well-configured network is also easier to troubleshoot, which brings a level of operational efficiency that every organization desires.

Network installation and configuration is a multifaceted discipline that serves as the backbone of all IT operations. Understanding the hardware aspects, grasping the importance of network services like DHCP and DNS, diving into the realms of virtualization and cloud computing, and adhering to best practices are all integral to becoming proficient in network setup and configuration.

Physical Network Setup

The physical setup of a network is a critical step in building a robust and efficient communication system. It involves the installation of various hardware components, setting up the network topology, and connecting all the devices so that they can communicate with each other. This chapter will provide a detailed overview of the significance of proper physical setup, types of networking cables, devices that make up a network, the different aspects of setting up a physical network, including the selection and installation of network devices, setting up the network topology, and ensuring the network is secure and efficient.

The Significance of Proper Physical Setup

The physical network setup goes beyond just connecting cables and turning on switches; it's the bedrock upon which the digital services and functionalities of your network reside. A well-planned and executed physical network minimizes latency, maximizes throughput, and most importantly, ensures reliability. Issues in the physical setup can manifest as intermittent connectivity, slow data transfer, or even complete network failure—problems no IT professional wants to grapple with. Therefore, let's delve into the components and best practices that constitute a robust physical network.

Networking Cables and Their Types

To begin, consider the veins and arteries of your network—the cables. Networking cables come in various types, each serving a particular purpose and environment. While Ethernet cables like Cat 5e, Cat 6, and Cat 7 are commonly used for local area networks (LANs), you might encounter fiber-optic cables for connections requiring higher speed and lower latency, such as in a data center. The choice of cable type can impact not only data transfer speeds but also the distance data can travel without degradation. Therefore, understanding the specific requirements of your network is crucial for selecting the appropriate cabling.

Devices That Make a Network

Next, let's turn our attention to the devices that make the network tick. These are the hubs, switches, routers, and firewalls. A hub is the most basic networking device that connects multiple computers in a network in a star topology. However, it's less commonly used today due to its limitations. Switches are more sophisticated, capable of learning and forwarding data only to the designated recipient, thereby optimizing network performance. Routers, on the other hand, are the traffic controllers, directing data between different networks including the vast frontier we call the internet. Firewalls act as the security guards, scrutinizing data packets to prevent unauthorized access. Knowing how to appropriately choose, configure, and deploy these devices is key to a successful network setup.

The Lay of the Land: Network Topology

The term "topology" refers to the layout of the various elements of your network—how they're interconnected and how they communicate. Choices range from star and ring to mesh and hybrid topologies, each with its advantages and disadvantages. For instance, a star topology might be easier to install and manage, but a mesh topology provides higher redundancy. The selection of a particular topology often depends on factors such as the scale of your network, the criticality of data flow, and the available budget.

Power, Redundancy, and Environmental Considerations

While not immediately obvious, ensuring stable power supply and adequate environmental conditions is critical to the physical network setup. Uninterruptible Power Supplies (UPS) are often deployed to provide a buffer in case of power failures. Redundancy, whether in the form of extra cables or backup devices, is often implemented to ensure network uptime. Environmental factors such as temperature and humidity can also impact the performance of networking equipment, which is why climate control is a consideration in data centers and server rooms.

It would be remiss not to address best practices in physical network setup. Proper cable management can save hours of troubleshooting down the line. Labeling cables and devices, maintaining a clean and organized environment, and documenting the network setup can make network management and future expansions considerably easier.

Selecting and Installing Network Devices

The first step in setting up a physical network is to select the appropriate network devices. These include switches, routers, firewalls, and other network appliances. Each of these devices plays a crucial role in the network, and it is important to select the right ones based on your network's requirements.

Switches: These devices are used to connect multiple devices on a local area network (LAN). They use MAC addresses to forward data to the correct device.

There are different types of switches, including managed and unmanaged switches. Managed switches allow you to configure settings and monitor the network, while unmanaged switches do not.

Routers: These devices are used to connect different networks, usually a local network to the internet. They use IP addresses to forward data packets between networks.

Firewalls: These devices are used to secure your network by filtering incoming and outgoing traffic based on a set of predefined rules.

Other network appliances: Depending on your network's requirements, you may need other devices such as load balancers, network-attached storage (NAS) devices, or wireless access points (WAPs).

Once you have selected the appropriate devices, the next step is to install them. This involves connecting the devices to each other and to the network. Make sure to follow the manufacturer's instructions carefully and test each device to ensure it is working correctly.

Setting Up the Network Topology

The network topology is the arrangement of the network devices and how they are connected to each other. There are several different topologies, each with its advantages and disadvantages.

Bus topology: In this topology, all devices are connected to a single central cable, known as the bus. It is simple and easy to set up but can lead to congestion and is not suitable for large networks.

Star topology: In this topology, all devices are connected to a central device, usually a switch or a hub. It is easy to add or remove devices, and a failure in one cable will not affect other devices. However, if the central device fails, the entire network will be affected.

Ring topology: In this topology, each device is connected to two other devices, forming a ring. It is more resilient than the bus topology, as data can travel in both directions, but it can be more complex to set up and manage.

Mesh topology: In this topology, devices are connected to multiple other devices. It is the most resilient topology, as there are multiple paths for data to travel, but it is also the most complex to set up and manage.

Hybrid topology: This is a combination of two or more different topologies.

When setting up the network topology, it is important to consider the network's requirements and select the topology that is best suited to your needs. Consider factors such as the number of devices, the amount of data traffic, and the need for redundancy and resilience.

Ensuring Network Security and Efficiency

Once the network devices have been installed and the topology set up, it is important to ensure that the network is secure and efficient. This involves configuring the devices, setting up security measures, and monitoring the network's performance.

Device configuration: Each network device needs to be configured to ensure it operates correctly and efficiently. This includes configuring the IP addresses, subnet masks, and default gateways on the routers and switches, setting up VLANs, and configuring the firewall rules.

Security measures: It is crucial to secure the network to prevent unauthorized access and data breaches. This includes setting up firewalls, configuring access controls, and implementing other security measures such as VPNs and intrusion detection systems (IDS).

Network monitoring: Regularly monitoring the network's performance is essential to ensure it is operating efficiently and to identify any potential problems before they become serious. This includes monitoring the network traffic, bandwidth usage, and device performance.

Setting up a physical network involves selecting and installing the network devices, setting up the network topology, and ensuring the network is secure and efficient. It is important to carefully consider the network's requirements and select the appropriate devices and topology. Once the network is set up, it is important to regularly monitor its performance and update the configuration and security measures as necessary.

LAN/WAN Technologies

Understanding the technologies that enable communication over local and wide areas is indispensable. LAN (Local Area Network) and WAN (Wide Area Network) technologies are the backbone of any organization's communication infrastructure, each fulfilling specific roles that are crucial to seamless connectivity. In this section, we will embark on an exploration of these technologies, demystifying their complexities and intricacies to prepare you for the CompTIA Network+ exam and your future career.

A Local Area Network, or LAN, is a network of devices that are located within a limited geographical area, such as a home, office, or campus. LANs are designed to enable the sharing of resources and information quickly and efficiently. Typically, LANs are used to connect personal computers, workstations, and servers to share resources like files, applications, and internet access.

Components of a LAN:

- Network Interface Cards (NICs): These are hardware devices that connect the computers to the network. Each NIC has a unique MAC address that identifies the device on the network.

- Switches: These are networking devices that manage data traffic efficiently by forwarding data only to specific devices on the network rather than to all devices within the LAN.

- Routers: These are devices that connect different networks. In a LAN, a router is used to connect the local network to the internet or to other LANs.

- Cabling and Connectors: These include the physical cables (e.g., Ethernet cables, fiber optics) and connectors that link all the devices on the network.

- Wireless Access Points: These are devices that allow wireless devices to connect to the network.

Ethernet is the most common LAN technology. It uses a protocol that controls the way packets of data are placed on the network. Ethernet is typically used in a star topology where each device on the network is connected to a central switch or hub.

Wide Area Networks (WANs)

A Wide Area Network, or WAN, interconnects LANs that are geographically separated, often across cities, states, or even countries. The internet is the most well-known WAN. WANs are used to transmit data over long distances, and can be either public or private. For example, a corporation with offices in different parts of the world may use a private WAN to connect its offices.

Components of a WAN:

- Routers: These are critical devices in a WAN as they direct data packets between the interconnected LANs.

- Modems: These are devices that modulate and demodulate digital signals to allow them to be transmitted over telephone lines or other long-distance media.

- Dedicated Lines: These are permanent connections between two locations. They offer a fixed bandwidth and are often used for high-volume data transmission, such as between data centers.

- Packet Switching: This is a method of data transmission where data is broken into packets and each packet is sent independently over the network. This is the most common method used in WANs.

- Circuit Switching: This is another method of data transmission where a dedicated communication path is established between two devices for the duration of their communication. This method is less common and is usually used for voice communication.

WAN technologies can be either leased lines, which are dedicated lines rented from a service provider, or broadband connections, which are shared lines that offer higher bandwidth.

Understanding LAN and WAN technologies is fundamental for any network professional and is a critical component of the CompTIA Network+ certification exam. This chapter provided a comprehensive and detailed overview of both LAN and WAN technologies, their components, and methods of data transmission.

Wireless Networks

The advent of wireless technology has revolutionized the way we communicate and share information. It has made connectivity more accessible, flexible, and convenient. Wireless networks are everywhere, from our homes and offices to public places like airports, hotels, and cafes. As a prospective CompTIA Network+ certified professional, it is imperative to have a thorough understanding of wireless networks, their components, configurations, and associated security challenges.

Components of Wireless Networks

Wireless networks comprise several components, each serving a specific function to ensure seamless communication and data transmission. At the core of any wireless network is the wireless access point (AP), a networking hardware device that allows a Wi-Fi enabled device to connect to a wired network. The AP acts as a bridge between the wired and wireless networks, enabling devices to communicate with each other and access the internet. Other essential components include wireless network adapters, wireless routers, and wireless range extenders.

- Wireless Network Adapters: These are hardware devices installed in computers or other devices to connect to a wireless network. Most modern devices come with built-in wireless network adapters, but external adapters can also be added via USB ports or other connections.

- Wireless Routers: These are devices that combine the functionality of a router and an access point. They direct traffic between devices on a local network and external networks like the internet. Wireless routers often include additional features like firewall protection, network address translation (NAT), and virtual private network (VPN) support.

- Wireless Range Extenders: These devices, also known as wireless repeaters, are used to extend the range of a wireless network. They receive wireless signals from an AP or router and retransmit them to areas where the signal is weak or non-existent.

Configuring Wireless Networks

Configuring a wireless network involves several steps and considerations to ensure optimal performance and security. Firstly, you must select the appropriate wireless standard for your network. The wireless standard, commonly referred to as Wi-Fi, has evolved over the years, with each new version offering improved speed, range, and security features. The most recent standard, as of my last update, is Wi-Fi 6 (802.11ax), which provides faster speeds and better performance in congested areas. However, both the AP or router and the connecting devices must support the same standard to take full advantage of its features.

Next, you must configure the wireless settings of the AP or router. These settings include the network name (SSID), the wireless channel, and the security settings. The SSID is the name of the wireless network and should be unique and easily identifiable. The wireless channel determines the frequency band used for communication between devices. It is essential to select a channel with minimal interference from other networks or electronic devices. Lastly, you must configure the security settings of the network. Security is a crucial aspect of wireless networks, as the wireless signals can be intercepted by unauthorized users. It is recommended to use the strongest encryption available, typically WPA3 (Wi-Fi Protected Access 3), and a strong passphrase to protect the network.

Wireless Network Security

Security is a paramount concern for wireless networks due to the nature of wireless communication. Unlike wired networks, where data is transmitted over physical cables, wireless networks transmit data over the air, making it susceptible to interception by unauthorized users. Several security measures must be implemented to safeguard the network:

- Encryption: This involves encoding the data transmitted between devices so that only authorized devices with the correct encryption key can decipher it. WPA3 is the latest and most secure encryption standard available.

- Authentication: This involves verifying the identity of devices or users attempting to connect to the network. It ensures that only authorized devices or users can access the network and its resources.

- MAC Address Filtering: This involves restricting access to the network based on the MAC (Media Access Control) address of the devices. Only devices with MAC addresses listed in the AP or router's allowed list can connect to the network.

- Firewall: This involves configuring the firewall settings of the AP or router to block unauthorized access to the network and protect against cyberattacks.

Understanding the components, configuration, and security of wireless networks is crucial for any network professional. Wireless networks offer convenience and flexibility but also pose unique security challenges that must be addressed to ensure a safe and secure communication environment. Implementing robust security measures like strong encryption, authentication, MAC address filtering, and a firewall will help protect the network from unauthorized access and cyberattacks.

Configuring Network Devices

The process of configuring network devices is a critical component of setting up a network. Network devices, such as routers, switches, and firewalls, are essential for establishing and managing network communications. Properly configuring these devices is crucial for the network's performance, security, and reliability. This chapter will provide a detailed overview of the key concepts and steps involved in configuring network devices, focusing on the knowledge required for the CompTIA Network+ certification exam.

Network Device Types

Before diving into the configuration details, it's important to have a clear understanding of the different types of network devices that you may encounter.

- **Routers**: These devices are responsible for forwarding data packets between different networks. Routers use routing tables and routing protocols to determine the most efficient path for data to travel from its source to its destination.

- **Switches**: Switches operate at the data link layer of the OSI model and are responsible for forwarding data frames within a local area network (LAN).

Switches use MAC addresses to determine the destination of a data frame and forward it only to the relevant port.

- **Firewalls**: Firewalls are security devices that monitor and filter incoming and outgoing network traffic based on an organization's security policies. Firewalls can be hardware-based or software-based and are essential for protecting a network from unauthorized access and cyberattacks.

Basic Configuration Tasks

When configuring network devices, there are several basic tasks that you will commonly encounter:

- **Setting Hostnames**: Assigning a meaningful hostname to a device makes it easier to identify and manage in a network. For example, a switch located in the server room of a company's headquarters might be named "HQ-ServerRoom-Switch1".

- **Assigning IP Addresses**: Devices such as routers and switches need to be assigned IP addresses to communicate over the network. This involves assigning an IP address and subnet mask to each interface on the device.

- **Configuring Routing**: For routers, you will need to configure routing protocols (such as OSPF or EIGRP) and static routes to enable communication between different networks.

- **Configuring VLANs**: On switches, you may need to configure Virtual Local Area Networks (VLANs) to segregate network traffic and improve security and performance.

- **Setting Passwords**: Setting strong passwords for accessing network devices is crucial for security. You should set passwords for console access, enable privileged mode, and remote access (such as SSH or Telnet).

Configuring Routers

Configuring a router involves several key steps:

1. **Accessing the Router**: First, you need to access the router's command-line interface (CLI) using a console cable or a remote access method such as SSH or Telnet.

2. **Entering Global Configuration Mode**: Once you have accessed the router's CLI, you need to enter global configuration mode by typing **configure terminal** or **conf t** for short.

3. **Configuring Interfaces**: Each interface on the router needs to be configured with an IP address and subnet mask. For example, to configure the IP address 192.168.1.1/24 on interface GigabitEthernet 0/0, you would enter the following commands:

```kotlin
interface GigabitEthernet0/0
ip address 192.168.1.1 255.255.255.0
no shutdown
```

4. **Configuring Routing**: To enable communication between different networks, you need to configure routing on the router. This involves configuring static routes or dynamic routing protocols. For example, to configure a static route to the network 192.168.2.0/24 with a next-hop IP address of 192.168.1.2, you would enter the following command:

```
ip route 192.168.2.0 255.255.255.0 192.168.1.2
```

5. **Saving the Configuration**: Once you have finished configuring the router, it is important to save the configuration to the device's non-volatile memory (NVRAM) so that it is not lost when the device is powered off or restarted. This can be done by entering the **write memory** or **copy running-config startup-config** command.

Configuring Switches

The process of configuring a switch is similar to configuring a router, but there are some key differences and additional steps involved:

1. **Accessing the Switch**: Similar to a router, you need to access the switch's CLI using a console cable or a remote access method such as SSH or Telnet.

2. **Entering Global Configuration Mode**: Enter global configuration mode by typing **configure terminal** or **conf t** for short.

3. **Configuring Interfaces**: Configure the IP address and subnet mask on the switch's management interface or VLAN interface. This allows the switch to be managed remotely over the network. For example, to configure the IP address 192.168.1.1/24 on VLAN 1, you would enter the following commands:

```kotlin
interface vlan 1
ip address 192.168.1.1 255.255.255.0
no shutdown
```

4. **Configuring VLANs**: VLANs are used to segregate network traffic and improve security and performance. To create a VLAN on a switch, enter the **vlan** command followed by the VLAN ID. For example, to create VLAN 10, you would enter the following command:

```
vlan 10
name Accounting
```

5. **Assigning Ports to VLANs**: After creating a VLAN, you need to assign ports to the VLAN. For example, to assign ports GigabitEthernet 0/1 to 0/10 to VLAN 10, you would enter the following commands:

```go
interface range GigabitEthernet0/1 - 10
switchport mode access
switchport access vlan 10
```

6. **Saving the Configuration**: Similar to a router, it is important to save the configuration to the device's NVRAM by entering the **write memory** or **copy running-config startup-config** command.

Configuring Firewalls

Configuring a firewall involves several key steps that differ from configuring switches and routers due to their focus on network security. Here is a general guideline on how to go about it:

1. **Accessing the Firewall**: Firewalls can usually be accessed through a Graphical User Interface (GUI), though some also offer command-line access. Secure Shell (SSH) is a common method for remote access.

2. **Initial Setup**: Most firewalls require an initial setup process, where you define the basic settings such as the firewall's IP address, subnet mask, and default gateway. These settings can often be configured through a setup wizard in the firewall's GUI.

3. **Defining Security Policies**: At the core of a firewall's functionality are its security policies. These policies dictate what kind of network traffic is allowed or disallowed. In most firewalls, you define rules that specify the source and destination IP addresses, protocols, and ports, along with an action (allow or deny).

4. **Configuring NAT and PAT**: Network Address Translation (NAT) and Port Address Translation (PAT) are commonly used on firewalls to map internal IP addresses to external IP addresses. This allows multiple devices on the internal network to share a single public IP address.

5. **Setting Up VPNs**: Virtual Private Networks (VPNs) are often configured on firewalls to allow secure, remote access to the internal network. This involves setting up VPN protocols, encryption algorithms, and authentication methods.

6. **Enabling Intrusion Detection and Prevention**: Many firewalls come with Intrusion Detection Systems (IDS) and Intrusion Prevention Systems (IPS) features that monitor network traffic for malicious activities. This involves defining what constitutes 'malicious' behavior and what actions should be taken when such behavior is detected.

7. **Logging and Monitoring**: It's crucial to set up logging on a firewall. Logging keeps a record of network activities and can be invaluable for troubleshooting and auditing purposes. Most firewalls also offer real-time

monitoring features, allowing you to observe the network traffic passing through the device in real time.

8. **Saving and Backup**: Similar to routers and switches, it's vital to save your configurations so they survive a reboot. It's also advisable to back up your configuration settings regularly and especially before making major changes.

9. **Testing**: After completing the configuration, rigorous testing is essential to ensure that the firewall is operating as expected. This can include penetration testing and monitoring for any unauthorized or unexpected activities.

10. **Maintaining**: Firewall configurations are not a 'set and forget' setting. They need to be reviewed and updated regularly to adapt to new security threats and organizational changes.

Configuring network devices is not just a technical task but a nuanced art that balances performance, reliability, and security. While routers are optimized to efficiently direct data between networks, switches aim to smoothly handle data within a network, and firewalls stand guard to ensure that all data crossing in and out meet the organization's security policies. A sound understanding of how to properly configure these devices is indispensable for anyone preparing for the CompTIA Network+ exam. And not only will this knowledge set you up for success in the exam, but it will also provide a solid foundation for real-world networking tasks you may encounter in your professional journey.

Virtualization and Cloud Computing

In the contemporary IT landscape, the paradigms of virtualization and cloud computing have emerged as transformative forces. The elasticity they offer in managing resources, coupled with cost efficiency, has made them indispensable components in network design and administration. As you are preparing for the CompTIA Network+ exam, it's essential to comprehend these two pivotal technologies, not merely as buzzwords but as practical solutions for today's increasingly complex networking challenges.

Virtualization: A Key to Resource Efficiency

Virtualization is the art of using software to create a simulated, or "virtual," environment that mimics a physical computing environment. It enables multiple operating systems and applications to share the resources of a single physical server, a feature that has profound implications for network design, testing, and management. In the context of the Network+ exam, understanding virtualization involves grasping its types, benefits, and potential security risks.

Let's talk about types first. You've got your full virtualization, para-virtualization, and hardware-assisted virtualization, each with its own use-cases and benefits. Full virtualization allows for the complete emulation of hardware, providing an all-encompassing environment where an operating system doesn't know it's running on a virtual machine. Para-virtualization, on the other hand, is more collaborative; the operating system is aware of the virtual environment and operates more efficiently as a result. Hardware-assisted virtualization leverages CPU features to assist in the virtualization process, offering improved performance.

Of course, the benefits are numerous. One of the most obvious is resource optimization. Virtualization allows you to utilize server capacity more efficiently, reducing hardware costs and power consumption. Additionally, it provides a level of agility and speed in deploying new applications, aiding in business continuity and disaster recovery.

However, with every rose comes its thorns. Security is a critical concern when implementing virtualization. Unauthorized access to the hypervisor, the software that creates and runs virtual machines, could potentially compromise all of the virtualized environments running on that host. Therefore, understanding the importance of securing the hypervisor, limiting user permissions, and implementing robust firewalls is vital for network security.

Cloud Computing: The Network Beyond Your Physical Walls

If virtualization is the stage, then cloud computing is the play. Cloud computing is the delivery of computing services over the internet, ranging from storage and databases to software, networking, and intelligence. For your CompTIA Network+ exam, a solid understanding of the different service models, deployment models, and the intrinsic link between cloud computing and networking is imperative.

There are primarily three service models to be familiar with:

- Infrastructure as a Service (IaaS)
- Platform as a Service (PaaS)
- Software as a Service (SaaS)

IaaS is essentially virtualized computing resources over the internet. PaaS provides a platform allowing customers to develop, run, and manage applications without dealing with the complexity of building and maintaining the infrastructure. SaaS, the most commonly used form, is a method for delivering software applications over the Internet, on-demand, and typically on a subscription basis.

Understanding the deployment models is equally critical. We have:

- Public Cloud
- Private Cloud
- Hybrid Cloud

The public cloud is owned and operated by third-party providers and delivers computing resources over the Internet. A private cloud refers to cloud computing resources used exclusively by a single organization. Hybrid clouds combine public and private clouds, allowing data to be shared between them.

And don't forget about networking in the cloud. It introduces new layers of complexity because you're dealing with distributed resources that may span different geographies and underlying technologies. Therefore, a robust understanding of how to set up and manage Virtual Private Networks (VPNs), application delivery controllers, and firewalls within the cloud is crucial.

Virtualization and cloud computing are more than just technological jargon; they are methodologies that can offer organizations unprecedented agility, cost savings, and scalability. For anyone aiming to ace the CompTIA Network+ exam, an in-depth understanding of these topics is not negotiable. They are an integral part of modern networking, affecting how resources are allocated, how data is stored and accessed, and how security protocols are implemented across both localized and distributed network environments.

DHCP and DNS Configuration

As we dive deeper into the world of networking, it is crucial to understand the importance of DHCP and DNS configuration. These are two essential services that ensure the proper functioning of any network. This chapter will provide a comprehensive understanding of what DHCP and DNS are, why they are important, and how to configure them effectively to ensure network stability and efficiency.

DHCP, or Dynamic Host Configuration Protocol, is a network management protocol used on IP networks. It automatically assigns IP addresses and other network configuration parameters to devices on a network. This eliminates the need for a network administrator to manually assign IP addresses to all network devices and allows for the recovery and reallocation of IP addresses.

DNS, or Domain Name System, is like the phonebook of the internet. It translates human-readable domain names (e.g., www.google.com) into IP addresses that are used by network devices to communicate with each other. Proper DNS configuration ensures that devices can accurately and quickly resolve domain names, which is critical for the functioning of the internet and intranet services.

Understanding DHCP

The DHCP service is essential for the dynamic allocation of network parameters to devices on a network. When a device is connected to a network, it sends a broadcast request for network configuration parameters. The DHCP server responds to this request by assigning an IP address from a predefined pool of addresses, along with other network parameters such as the subnet mask, default gateway, and DNS servers.

Key components of DHCP include:

- DHCP Client: A device that requests network configuration parameters from a DHCP server.

- DHCP Server: A server that holds a pool of IP addresses and other network parameters and assigns them to DHCP clients upon request.

- IP Address Pool: A range of IP addresses that the DHCP server can assign to clients.

- Lease: The length of time for which an IP address is assigned to a DHCP client. When the lease expires, the client must request a new IP address.

Configuring DHCP

Configuring a DHCP server involves defining the range of IP addresses to be assigned to clients (the IP address pool), the lease duration, and other network parameters. Here is a step-by-step guide to configuring a DHCP server:

1. Install the DHCP Server: Install the DHCP server software on a server or a network device that will act as the DHCP server.

2. Define the IP Address Pool: Define the range of IP addresses that the DHCP server will assign to clients. Make sure that the range does not overlap with any static IP addresses assigned to network devices.

3. Set the Lease Duration: Define the length of time for which an IP address will be assigned to a client. A typical lease duration is 24 hours.

4. Configure Other Network Parameters: Define other network parameters such as the default gateway, DNS servers, and subnet mask.

5. Start the DHCP Server: Start the DHCP server service and monitor the logs to ensure that it is running correctly.

Understanding DNS

DNS is a hierarchical and decentralized naming system for computers, services, or other resources connected to the internet or a private network. It translates human-readable domain names into machine-readable IP addresses. For example, when you type "www.openai.com" into your web browser, the DNS system translates this into an IP address that your computer can use to access the OpenAI website.

Key components of DNS include:

- Domain Name: A human-readable name that represents an IP address on the internet (e.g., openai.com).

- DNS Server: A server that holds a database of domain names and their corresponding IP addresses. It resolves domain name queries into IP addresses.

- Resolver: A DNS client that requests DNS servers to resolve domain names into IP addresses.

- Root Server: A DNS server that knows the IP addresses of all the top-level domain (TLD) servers. It is the first step in translating domain names into IP addresses.

Configuring DNS

Configuring a DNS server involves defining the domain names and their corresponding IP addresses. Here is a step-by-step guide to configuring a DNS server:

1. Install the DNS Server: Install the DNS server software on a server or a network device that will act as the DNS server.

2. Define the Domain Names: Define the domain names and their corresponding IP addresses. This can be done by creating DNS records. There are several types of DNS records, such as A (Address Record), CNAME (Canonical Name Record), and MX (Mail Exchange Record).

3. Configure Forwarders: A forwarder is a DNS server that is used to forward DNS queries that cannot be resolved locally to other DNS servers on the internet. Configure the DNS server to forward unresolved queries to a trusted DNS server, such as the DNS server of your internet service provider or a public DNS server.

4. Start the DNS Server: Start the DNS server service and monitor the logs to ensure that it is running correctly.

DHCP and DNS are two critical services that ensure the proper functioning of any network. A properly configured DHCP server ensures that devices on a network can communicate with each other by assigning them unique IP addresses. A properly configured DNS server ensures that devices can accurately and quickly resolve domain names into IP addresses, which is critical for accessing internet and intranet services.

Chapter 3: Network Media and Topologies

The foundation of any network lies in its media and topology. The media refers to the physical means through which data travels from one device to another, while the topology refers to the arrangement of these devices and the connections between them. Together, the media and topology determine the performance, reliability, and scalability of the network.

Understanding network media and topologies is crucial for designing, implementing, and troubleshooting networks. This chapter provides an overview of the different types of network media and common network topologies. Each type of media and topology has its own advantages and disadvantages, and the choice depends on various factors such as the size of the network, the required performance, and the budget.

Cable Types and Connectors

In the world of networking, the physical components are as critical as the virtual ones. The cables and connectors form the lifeline of a network, facilitating the transmission of data between various devices. Understanding the different types of cables and connectors is pivotal for any network professional, not only for the CompTIA Network+ certification exam but also for real-world applications. This chapter will provide a comprehensive overview of the most common cable types and connectors used in networking.

Copper Cables

Copper cables are the most traditional and widely used type of networking cable. These cables consist of copper wires that transmit electrical signals.

There are various types of copper cables, each designed for specific networking needs.

- Twisted Pair Cables: These are the most common type of networking cables. They consist of pairs of copper wires twisted together. The twisting helps to reduce electromagnetic interference (EMI) and crosstalk between adjacent pairs. Twisted pair cables come in two main categories:
- Unshielded Twisted Pair (UTP): UTP cables are the most popular twisted pair cables used for networking. They consist of color-coded pairs of copper wires

twisted together and enclosed in a plastic insulation. UTP cables are cost-effective and easy to install. They are commonly used for local area networks (LANs).

- Shielded Twisted Pair (STP): STP cables are similar to UTP cables, but they have an additional layer of metal foil or braided mesh that encases the pairs of wires. This additional shielding helps to protect the signals from external interference and makes STP cables suitable for environments with a high level of electromagnetic interference.

2. Coaxial Cables: Coaxial cables, commonly referred to as coax cables, consist of a single copper conductor surrounded by a layer of insulation, a metal shield, and an outer layer of insulation. The metal shield helps to protect the signal from external interference. Coaxial cables are commonly used for cable television, internet connections, and other data communication applications.

Fiber Optic Cables
Fiber optic cables are a more modern alternative to copper cables. They use light signals to transmit data, which allows for higher data transfer rates and longer transmission distances. Fiber optic cables consist of a core made of glass or plastic, surrounded by a cladding layer and an outer protective layer.

There are two main types of fiber optic cables:
1. Single-mode Fiber: Single-mode fiber cables have a small core diameter, usually around 9 microns. They are designed to carry light signals over long distances with minimal signal loss. Single-mode fiber cables are commonly used for backbone networks and long-distance data transmission.
2. Multi-mode Fiber: Multi-mode fiber cables have a larger core diameter, usually around 50 or 62.5 microns. They are designed to carry multiple light signals over shorter distances. Multi-mode fiber cables are commonly used for LANs and other short-distance applications.

Connectors
Connectors are used to connect cables to networking devices or other cables. There are various types of connectors used in networking, each designed for specific cable types and applications.
1. RJ-45: The RJ-45 connector is the most common connector used in networking. It is used to connect twisted pair cables, such as UTP and STP, to

networking devices like switches, routers, and computers. The RJ-45 connector has eight pins and is often referred to as an Ethernet connector.

2. RJ-11: The RJ-11 connector is similar to the RJ-45 connector, but it has only four or six pins. It is commonly used for telephone lines and other low-speed data connections.

3. SC: The SC connector, or Standard Connector, is a common fiber optic connector used for single-mode and multi-mode fiber cables. It has a push-pull coupling mechanism and is known for its durability and low cost.

4. LC: The LC connector, or Lucent Connector, is a smaller and more modern alternative to the SC connector. It has a latch coupling mechanism and is commonly used for high-density applications.

5. ST: The ST connector, or Straight Tip connector, is one of the oldest fiber optic connectors. It has a bayonet coupling mechanism and is commonly used for single-mode fiber cables.

Understanding the different types of cables and connectors is crucial for any network professional. It is essential to select the appropriate cables and connectors for each application to ensure the optimal performance and reliability of the network. Whether you are preparing for the CompTIA Network+ certification exam or working in the field, this knowledge will serve as a valuable foundation for your networking career.

Network Architecture (Ethernet, Token Ring, etc.)

Network architecture is the skeletal framework that holds together the entire body of a network, shaping how data flows, how devices connect, and how we interact with this intricate system. It is the blueprint that enables seamless communication between diverse hardware and software components. This chapter aims to explore the many facets of network architecture, including Ethernet protocols, token ring networks, and the role of switches and routers in modern networking environments. As you journey through this chapter, you'll find essential knowledge and nuanced insights that are crucial for anyone aspiring to excel in the CompTIA Network+ certification exam.

Ethernet Protocols

As we step into the realm of network architecture, Ethernet is often the first word that springs to mind. Ethernet is the most widely adopted network architecture and has evolved significantly since its inception in the late 1970s. Understanding Ethernet is crucial, not only because it's ubiquitous but also due to its foundational role in modern networking. In an Ethernet network, devices communicate using frames, encapsulated packets of data that contain source and destination MAC addresses.

Speed and performance are paramount in today's fast-paced environments. Ethernet networks have evolved to support varying speeds—from the legacy 10 Mbps to 100 Mbps, 1 Gbps, and even beyond to 10 Gbps and more. Understanding these variations is key to grasping how different Ethernet networks can be optimized for performance and cost-effectiveness.

Token Ring Networks

While Ethernet has become the de facto standard for local area networks, it is essential to be aware of other architectures like the Token Ring, even though they might seem archaic or less common. In a Token Ring network, data packets circulate in a logical ring, and only the device possessing the "token" can transmit data at any given time. This reduces collisions and can result in more predictable network performance compared to Ethernet.

One might question the relevance of studying Token Ring in today's Ethernet-dominated landscape. The answer lies in the versatility expected of a networking professional. You may encounter legacy systems in certain enterprise environments or specific use-cases where Token Ring's characteristics offer distinct advantages. Your thorough understanding of diverse network architectures, including Token Ring, will make you a more adaptable and resourceful network professional.

Switches and Routers

Moving from the logical to the physical elements of network architecture, switches and routers are indispensable components that govern data flow. While both perform the critical task of directing network traffic, they operate at different layers of the OSI model and serve distinct functions.

- **Switches**: Operate primarily at Layer 2 (Data Link Layer) and are adept at forwarding frames based on MAC addresses. They excel at creating collision domains, effectively isolating network segments to enhance performance.

- **Routers**: Function at Layer 3 (Network Layer) and make decisions based on IP addresses. Routers are the maestros of subnetting, directing data packets between different networks and even facilitating communication across the internet.

Recognizing the roles that switches and routers play in network architecture is vital for network planning, troubleshooting, and optimization. Their functions might seem straightforward, but mastering their subtleties will provide you with the skills to design more efficient and secure networks.

Network architecture is a multifaceted domain, and its understanding is instrumental for anyone aiming to become CompTIA Network+ certified. From Ethernet protocols to Token Ring networks and the indispensable roles of switches and routers, each component adds a unique layer of complexity and functionality to network design and operation.

Switching and Routing

Switching and routing are the cornerstones of network communications. They serve as the roads and highways that direct data traffic, ensuring that information reaches its intended destination efficiently and securely. Understanding the fundamental principles and practices of switching and routing is critical for anyone preparing for the CompTIA Network+ certification exam. In this chapter, we will embark on a deep dive into the realm of these two vital network functions, demystifying their operations and highlighting their relevance in modern networking.

Switching, to begin, is the process of directing data packets between devices on the same local network. The switch functions like a traffic controller, identifying devices using their Media Access Control (MAC) addresses and sending packets only to the intended recipients. This is especially crucial in enterprise environments where hundreds or even thousands of devices could be connected to the same network. By facilitating a targeted delivery mechanism, switches not only reduce network congestion but also enhance security by mitigating the risk of data eavesdropping.

Let's move from the immediate environs of a local network to the larger expanse of interconnected networks that make up the internet. Here, routing comes into play. Unlike switches, routers operate at a higher layer of the OSI model and make decisions based on the IP addresses. They serve as the custodians of data traffic between different networks, deciding the most efficient path for packets to travel from their source to their destination. Imagine you're sending an email from New York to a colleague in Tokyo; it's the router that determines how that email traverses the multiple networks between the two cities.

If you consider switching as operating within a neighborhood, routing is like the interstate highways connecting different cities. The router examines the destination IP address of each packet and consults its routing table—a sort of map—to determine the best way to forward it. To build this routing table, routers communicate with each other using routing protocols like RIP (Routing Information Protocol) and OSPF (Open Shortest Path First). These protocols update the router about changes in the network topology, ensuring that data always takes the most efficient route.

Now, one might wonder, "Why do we even need both switching and routing?" The answer lies in network optimization. Switching is incredibly efficient for local traffic and minimizes the load on the router. The router, in turn, focuses on directing traffic between different networks, ensuring that each plays to its strength. This separation of duties results in a more streamlined, efficient, and secure networking environment.

With the rise of software-defined networking (SDN) and network virtualization, the lines between switching and routing have started to blur. In modern networks, these functions can sometimes be managed through software, giving network administrators more flexibility and control. This development highlights the need for a robust understanding of both concepts, as they are continually evolving.

While switches and routers come with their set of configurations and commands, understanding their core functions is crucial. So, when you face questions in the CompTIA Network+ exam that ask you to troubleshoot connectivity issues or optimize a network layout, you'll know to consider the roles of switches and routers in the problem presented.

VLANs and Subnetting

When it comes to optimizing network performance and enhancing security, the concepts of VLANs (Virtual Local Area Networks) and subnetting are crucial tools in a network administrator's arsenal. These techniques empower professionals to manage traffic more efficiently and segment their networks to better align with organizational goals. In this chapter, we'll delve deep into the nuts and bolts of VLANs and subnetting, elucidating how they work, why they're important, and how they can be configured and applied in various networking scenarios.

Virtual Local Area Networks (VLANs)

Let's kick things off with VLANs. In a traditional LAN setup, all devices are part of the same broadcast domain. This means that broadcast messages, intended or not, go to every device on that network. VLANs effectively create isolated islands within a physical network, each behaving as a separate entity or a distinct broadcast domain. This isolation boosts security and improves network efficiency by restricting broadcasts to a smaller group of devices.

In a corporate environment, VLANs can be exceptionally useful. For instance, the finance and human resources departments can be placed in separate VLANs to add an extra layer of security and minimize the chance of unauthorized data access. To implement VLANs, one typically uses switches that support VLAN tagging, usually conforming to the IEEE 802.1Q standard.

One significant aspect of VLANs is the use of VLAN IDs. When a packet arrives at a VLAN-enabled switch, a tag indicating the VLAN ID is attached to the packet's header. This ID helps the switch determine how to route the packet and which ports can participate in that particular VLAN.

Subnetting

If VLANs are like different neighborhoods within a city, think of subnetting as the meticulous planning of roads, plots, and blocks within each neighborhood. In essence, subnetting is the technique used to divide an IP network into multiple, smaller network segments or "subnets."

Subnetting serves several essential purposes. For starters, it enhances routing efficiency. By breaking a large network into smaller subnets, routers have to manage fewer routes. This increases the speed and performance of the network. Secondly, subnetting can aid in security by making it easier to implement security policies for distinct segments of a network. Lastly, it allows for better control over IP address allocation, ensuring optimal use of a limited resource.

The concept of a 'subnet mask' is central to subnetting. This 32-bit number helps in distinguishing the network portion of an IP address from the host portion. For instance, in the IP address 192.168.1.1 with a subnet mask of 255.255.255.0, the '192.168.1' is the network part, and the '.1' is the host part. The subnet mask makes it easier for routers to know where to forward packets.

Melding VLANs and Subnetting

At first glance, VLANs and subnetting may appear to serve similar purposes, but they operate at different layers of the OSI model. VLANs function at the data link layer (Layer 2) while subnetting operates at the network layer (Layer 3). However, they often complement each other beautifully. For instance, a common practice is to assign a unique subnet to each VLAN, enhancing the overall organizational scheme and making the network easier to manage.

In configuring VLANs and subnets, planning is crucial. A poorly designed network can result in inefficiencies, bottlenecks, and security vulnerabilities. Network administrators usually deploy network management software that allows them to visualize the entire setup, facilitating the process of assigning VLAN IDs and subnet masks.

To sum it all up, VLANs and subnetting are two distinct but synergistic technologies that every aspiring network professional should master. By offering the capability to segment networks both physically and logically, these techniques provide a dual-layered approach to improving network efficiency, security, and manageability.

Chapter 4: Network Operations

The vitality of any network lies not just in its initial setup but in its ongoing operations. Network Operations is a multidimensional task, covering everything from the monitoring of network performance to configuration management, documentation, and disaster recovery. In this chapter, we will dissect each of these aspects to equip you with the knowledge and skills required to manage and maintain a network effectively, ensuring not only the flow of data but also the resilience and security that modern businesses demand.

Network Monitoring

The heartbeat of any IT environment is its network. When we consider the complexity of today's interconnected systems—servers, workstations, IoT devices, and more—it's evident how crucial the health of the network is. Imagine running a hospital with no pulse monitors or a city with no traffic lights. That's what an IT infrastructure would be like without network monitoring. This chapter digs deep into the nuances of network monitoring, a subject that holds immense importance, not only for day-to-day operational stability but also for long-term strategic planning.

The What and Why of Network Monitoring

Network monitoring is essentially the continuous observation of a network's performance to detect slow or failing components and to alert the network administrator of such occurrences. The goal isn't merely to identify issues but also to understand performance metrics and usage patterns. So, why is network monitoring important?

Firstly, in a reactive environment, troubleshooting network issues can be like finding a needle in a haystack. Network monitoring tools provide real-time information that can significantly reduce the time it takes to identify and resolve issues, ultimately improving the quality of service.

Secondly, network monitoring can provide invaluable data for planning infrastructure upgrades. Through performance metrics and usage statistics, administrators can identify bottlenecks and forecast future needs. This proactive approach ensures that the network can handle growth efficiently, without performance degradation or downtime.

Metrics Matter

When it comes to network monitoring, several metrics demand attention:

- **Bandwidth:** Monitoring bandwidth helps in ensuring that you're making the most of your network's capacity. It helps to avoid congestion and ensures that critical business applications have the bandwidth they need.
- **Latency:** High latency is often a sign of network congestion, hardware issues, or configuration errors. Monitoring latency can help you ensure that data is being transmitted efficiently across your network.
- **Packet Loss:** Frequent packet loss can severely degrade network performance and user experience. Monitoring packet loss can alert you to issues that may require immediate attention, such as faulty hardware or a saturated network link.
- **Error Rates:** Monitoring the rate of CRC errors, dropped packets, and other anomalies can provide a wealth of information about network health. High error rates often point to problems that need immediate correction.

The Tools of the Trade

Technology has blessed us with a wide array of network monitoring tools, each with its unique set of features. From open-source solutions like Nagios to commercial products like SolarWinds, these tools offer different methods for collecting data, setting alerts, and generating reports. The choice of a network monitoring tool often depends on your specific needs, the size and complexity of your network, and your budget constraints.

Once you have reliable monitoring in place, the next step is to define what actions to take when specific thresholds are crossed. Is an email notification enough, or is an immediate automated corrective action required? Deciding the appropriate response in advance is crucial for effective network management.

While real-time alerts and immediate corrective actions are tactical components of network monitoring, let's not forget the strategic aspect. The data collected through network monitoring can be analyzed to discern trends, which can then be used for long-term planning.

In conclusion, network monitoring isn't a luxury or an afterthought; it's a necessity. It provides the insights needed to manage complex networks effectively, ensuring not only the resolution of immediate issues but also aiding in strategic long-term planning.

Configuration Management

As the complexity of networking environments continues to grow, the need for an organized approach to managing configurations becomes increasingly vital. Configuration Management, a discipline that often forms the cornerstone of a well-maintained network, emerges as a requisite subject matter for professionals aiming for the CompTIA Network+ certification. In this chapter, we'll delve into the intricacies of Configuration Management, not just as a theoretical concept but as a pragmatic set of practices and tools that every network administrator must be proficient in.

Let's begin by demystifying what Configuration Management is. At its core, Configuration Management involves the systematic process of administering, updating, and auditing network configurations. While this might seem straightforward, the web of interdependencies, protocols, and services in modern networks make it a high-stakes operation. The smallest mistake in a configuration file could take down an entire network or expose it to severe security vulnerabilities. Therefore, Configuration Management is not just about altering settings but ensuring that these changes align with established guidelines and don't disrupt existing operations.

As part of Configuration Management, network administrators are often tasked with standardization. This involves creating baseline configurations that serve as a model for setting up new devices or updating existing ones. Standardization offers numerous benefits:

- Streamlines administrative tasks
- Facilitates rapid troubleshooting
- Helps in compliance with internal policies and external regulations

One of the critical components of Configuration Management is version control. When multiple individuals have the authority to alter network settings, the lack of a centralized tracking system can result in chaos. Version control tools log changes, helping administrators revert to previous configurations in case of errors or security incidents. These tools can also help in auditing, another vital aspect of

Configuration Management, which involves periodic checks to ensure configurations meet set standards and policies. In the modern landscape, where regulations like GDPR and HIPAA dictate stringent requirements, auditing is not just good practice but often a legal necessity.

Beyond just tools and practices, Configuration Management is about building a culture of responsibility and accountability. Every change, no matter how minor, should be documented meticulously. This practice of maintaining comprehensive documentation serves multiple purposes:

- Simplifies the process of troubleshooting
- Aids in training new staff
- Provides a historical context for configuration changes

Perhaps one of the most overlooked but essential aspects of Configuration Management is disaster recovery. Often, people assume that having backups suffices. However, backups are only as good as your ability to restore them effectively. This is where Configuration Management shines. By maintaining an up-to-date library of configurations and changes, network administrators can quickly restore services in the event of a failure, minimizing downtime and its associated costs.

Finally, let's touch upon the relationship between Configuration Management and security. When configurations are not properly managed, the risk of unauthorized access or data breaches escalates exponentially. An effective Configuration Management strategy incorporates security best practices, ensuring not just the functionality but also the integrity and safety of the network.

Network Documentation

Network documentation serves as the blueprint and historical record of the network, outlining its design, configuration, and modifications over time. For professionals aspiring to ace the CompTIA Network+ certification exam, understanding the importance of network documentation, its components, and best practices is essential. This chapter aims to provide a comprehensive overview of network documentation and its significance in ensuring the efficient operation, maintenance, and troubleshooting of a network.

Importance of Network Documentation

Network documentation is a critical aspect of managing and maintaining a network. It serves as a reference guide for network administrators, engineers, and other IT professionals involved in the network's operation and maintenance. Here are some key reasons why network documentation is essential:

1. Troubleshooting: Detailed network documentation helps in identifying and resolving network issues quickly. It provides a clear picture of the network's layout, configurations, and interconnections, making it easier to pinpoint problems and implement solutions.

2. Network Optimization: Network documentation helps in analyzing the network's performance and identifying areas for improvement. It provides a baseline for comparing the current network state with past configurations, helping in optimizing the network for better performance.

3. Disaster Recovery: In the event of a network failure or disaster, network documentation serves as a roadmap for restoring the network to its previous state. It outlines the network's design, configuration, and key components, making it easier to rebuild the network and recover lost data.

4. Change Management: Network documentation provides a historical record of changes made to the network. It helps in tracking modifications, identifying the impact of changes, and ensuring that changes are implemented correctly and do not adversely affect the network's operation.

5. Compliance: Many organizations are required to adhere to specific standards and regulations, such as GDPR or HIPAA. Network documentation helps in demonstrating compliance by providing a detailed record of the network's design, configuration, and security measures.

Components of Network Documentation

Network documentation comprises various components, each serving a specific purpose and contributing to the overall understanding and management of the network. Here are some key components of network documentation:

1. Network Topology: This is a visual representation of the network, showing the interconnections between devices, such as routers, switches, and servers. It includes both the physical topology, which represents the actual layout of devices and connections, and the logical topology, which represents the path data takes through the network.

2. Device Inventory: This is a list of all network devices, including their make, model, serial number, IP address, and location. It helps in identifying and

managing devices, tracking their status, and planning for upgrades or replacements.

3. IP Addressing Scheme: This outlines the IP addresses assigned to each device on the network. It includes details such as subnets, VLANs, and routing information, helping in managing IP addresses and ensuring efficient data transmission across the network.

4. Configuration Files: These are the files that contain the configuration settings of network devices, such as routers and switches. They include settings for routing, security, and device management, helping in configuring devices and restoring their configuration in case of failure.

5. Network Diagrams: These are visual representations of the network, showing the interconnections between devices and their logical relationships. They include details such as IP addresses, VLANs, and subnets, helping in understanding the network's layout and data flow.

Best Practices for Network Documentation

Creating and maintaining network documentation is a critical task that requires attention to detail and a systematic approach. Here are some best practices for network documentation:

1. Keep it Updated: Network documentation should be updated regularly to reflect changes in the network, such as the addition of new devices, changes in IP addresses, or modifications to configurations. Regular updates ensure that the documentation remains accurate and useful.

2. Be Detailed: Network documentation should be as detailed as possible, including all relevant information about the network, its devices, and configurations. Detailed documentation helps in understanding the network better and facilitates troubleshooting and maintenance.

3. Use Standardized Formats: Network documentation should be created and maintained in standardized formats, such as PDF or Microsoft Word, to ensure accessibility and compatibility across different platforms and devices.

4. Include Visuals: Visuals, such as network diagrams and topology maps, help in understanding the network's layout and data flow better. They should be included in the network documentation along with detailed explanations.

5. Secure the Documentation: Network documentation contains sensitive information about the network, such as IP addresses, configurations, and security settings. It should be stored securely, with access restricted to authorized personnel only.

Network documentation is a critical component of network management and maintenance. It serves as a reference guide for IT professionals, helping in troubleshooting, network optimization, disaster recovery, change management, and compliance. Proper network documentation includes various components, such as network topology, device inventory, IP addressing scheme, configuration files, and network diagrams. Following best practices for network documentation, such as keeping it updated, being detailed, using standardized formats, including visuals, and securing the documentation, ensures its usefulness and effectiveness.

Disaster Recovery and Business Continuity

Despite our best efforts to create robust and resilient systems, the truth remains: disasters happen. These can be natural, like hurricanes and floods, or human-made, such as cyberattacks or simple human error. The purpose of this chapter is to delve deeply into these two interrelated areas, emphasizing their importance not only for passing your CompTIA Network+ exam but also for excelling in any networking role.

Understanding the Importance of Disaster Recovery

Let's start by talking about disaster recovery. You can think of this as the emergency medical team that comes onto the field when an athlete gets injured—immediate, focused action to deal with a critical situation. Disaster recovery is the set of policies and procedures designed to quickly restore essential data and functions in the event of an emergency. This could be something as simple as a disk failure or as complex as a catastrophic natural disaster affecting an entire geographic region. The key elements of disaster recovery involve identifying critical systems, setting up backup procedures, and ensuring rapid restoration capabilities.

The Components of a Disaster Recovery Plan

A well-crafted disaster recovery plan typically involves several critical components, each designed to address different facets of the recovery process.

- Risk Assessment: Identifying vulnerabilities and the possible disasters that could exploit them.

- Recovery Objectives: Defining objectives like Recovery Point Objective (RPO) and Recovery Time Objective (RTO), which dictate how much data loss is acceptable and how quickly services must be restored.

- Communication Plan: Detailing how to disseminate information during and after a disaster, including who is responsible for each type of communication.

- Backup Solutions: Implementing technologies for data backup such as off-site storage, cloud backups, and redundant systems.

- Testing: Regularly validating the disaster recovery plan through drills and simulations to ensure its effectiveness.

Business Continuity: The Larger Picture

While disaster recovery focuses on immediate response and restoration, business continuity is the grand strategy—the game plan for how your organization will continue its critical functions during and after a disaster. It involves more than just technology; it includes human resources, facilities, and external contacts like suppliers and customers. It's about ensuring that disruptions have as little impact as possible on the operational flow of a business.

Key Elements of a Business Continuity Plan

Just like with disaster recovery, a business continuity plan isn't a one-size-fits-all template but should be customized to fit the specific needs and nuances of an organization. However, common elements often include:

- Business Impact Analysis: Identifying the functions and related resources that are time-sensitive.

- Continuity Strategies: Planning for resource allocation and process management during a disaster.

- Employee Training: Ensuring that staff knows what to do in case of an emergency, including how to use backup systems and who to contact.

- Vendor Management: Establishing relationships with third parties that may be required for quick response and recovery.

- Regular Updates: Constantly revisiting and updating the business continuity plan to adapt to new challenges and technologies.

The Symbiotic Relationship

At first glance, disaster recovery and business continuity might seem like two entirely different practices, but they are deeply interconnected. Business continuity can't exist without a robust disaster recovery plan, and disaster recovery is most effective when it's part of a broader business continuity strategy. Together, they form a comprehensive approach to risk management, ensuring not just the survival but the thriving of an organization in the face of adversity.

In preparation for the CompTIA Network+ exam, it's essential to understand both the theoretical and practical aspects of these topics. Disaster recovery and business continuity questions often appear on the exam, not just as standalone questions but also as parts of broader networking scenarios that test your overall understanding of network management and sustainability.

SLAs and Quality of Service

A Service Level Agreement (SLA) is one of the most potent tools in ensuring that the quality of service (QoS) meets or exceeds the required standards. An SLA is a contractual commitment between a service provider and a client, delineating the scope, quality, and responsibilities of the service to be provided. Understanding SLAs and the concept of Quality of Service is crucial for anyone aiming to excel in the CompTIA Network+ exam and, by extension, in their IT career.

Understanding SLAs

An SLA is often compared to a blueprint or a roadmap for service expectations. When you're managing or administering a network, you're essentially providing a service, and an SLA outlines the expectations for that service. It contains metrics like uptime, bandwidth, latency, and other key performance indicators (KPIs) that the service must meet. But an SLA is more than a list of metrics; it's a legal document that stipulates penalties for failing to meet the agreed-upon standards. This lends a level of gravity to SLAs that extends beyond mere promises or verbal agreements.

Understanding SLAs isn't just about knowing what the acronyms stand for; it's about grasping the operational, financial, and legal implications of these agreements. For example, an SLA may require that network downtime doesn't exceed 5 hours a month. Failure to meet this could result in financial penalties for the service provider, not to mention the potential loss of client trust and future business opportunities.

Quality of Service: More Than a Buzzword

Moving on to Quality of Service (QoS), it's easy to dismiss this as a buzzword that gets tossed around in networking circles. However, QoS is an integral part of modern networking practices that directly influences the effectiveness of an SLA. At its core, QoS involves prioritizing network resources by controlling packet loss, delay, and jitter, thereby ensuring that the service remains consistent and reliable.

In practical terms, QoS is implemented through a range of methods and technologies. These might include configuring priority queues for essential applications or services, or using rate limiting to prevent non-essential applications from hogging bandwidth. By managing these aspects, you're essentially ensuring that all applications receive the network resources they require, thereby fulfilling the service expectations outlined in your SLA.

Linking SLAs and QoS

So, how do SLAs and QoS relate to each other? Essentially, an SLA provides a framework for QoS. The SLA sets the standards, and QoS mechanisms help in achieving those standards. If an SLA sets a certain latency or uptime rate, various QoS techniques are employed to meet these benchmarks. Failure to properly implement QoS can result in SLA breaches, leading to those aforementioned financial penalties and reputational damage. Therefore, mastering the concepts and practical applications of both SLAs and QoS is imperative for anyone in the network field and will constitute a significant part of your CompTIA Network+ exam.

Best Practices for SLAs and QoS

There are some fundamental best practices to follow when dealing with SLAs and QoS:

Always negotiate SLAs rather than accepting predefined templates. This ensures that both parties' needs and capacities are considered.

Regularly review and update SLAs to reflect changes in technology, business goals, or customer needs.

Implement monitoring tools that can actively measure QoS metrics in real-time, allowing for immediate corrective action.

By internalizing these best practices, you not only increase your chances of acing the CompTIA Network+ exam but also add invaluable skills to your professional toolkit.

In summary, SLAs and Quality of Service are more than just terminologies or checkboxes to tick off in your network administration responsibilities. They are foundational principles that will guide you in your journey towards becoming a network professional of repute. Armed with a comprehensive understanding of these topics, you'll be better prepared to handle the challenges posed by the CompTIA Network+ exam and beyond.

Chapter 5: Network Security

In an age where data breaches, cyberattacks, and hacking attempts make headlines almost every day, network security emerges as the linchpin of any organization's technological infrastructure. In this chapter, we'll explore how to secure a network, with a focus on real-world applications that directly relate to the CompTIA Network+ certification exam.

When most people think about network security, their minds often jump to firewalls and antivirus software. While these are crucial elements, network security is a multifaceted discipline that begins with understanding the basic concepts. At its core, network security aims to protect the integrity, confidentiality, and availability of data as it is stored, processed, and transferred across a network. Often abbreviated as the CIA triad, these three pillars lay the groundwork for any secure network.

Once you've wrapped your mind around the CIA triad, the next focus should naturally shift to understanding the hardware and software solutions that come into play. Firewalls and Intrusion Detection Systems (IDS) or Intrusion Prevention Systems (IPS) serve as the guardians of a network. Firewalls act as filters between your network and external networks like the internet. They are rule-based systems that allow or deny traffic based on predefined security policies. On the other hand, IDS/IPS systems are more proactive, scanning for patterns in network traffic that might indicate a security threat. Mastering the configuration, deployment, and maintenance of these tools is a core skill for any network security professional.

The narrative of network security also encompasses Virtual Private Networks (VPNs) and remote access. In a world where remote work and distributed teams are increasingly common, ensuring secure remote access to a network is of paramount importance. VPNs allow users to connect to a network securely over the internet by encrypting all data traffic. If configured correctly, VPNs can ensure that remote workers have the same level of access and security as those physically present in the office.

Another aspect that often gets overshadowed in discussions about network security is wireless security. Unlike wired networks, wireless networks transmit data over radio waves, making them inherently more susceptible to interception.

Technologies like WPA3 and the use of strong authentication methods can substantially mitigate these risks. From understanding the different types of wireless encryption to knowing how to set up a secure wireless access point, grasping the fundamentals of wireless security can go a long way in preventing unauthorized access to your network.

However, technology alone is not enough to secure a network. This is where the role of security policies and compliance frameworks comes in. Whether it's setting up user permissions or conducting regular security audits, these written guidelines serve as the roadmap for an organization's security strategy. This is also where you would consider compliance with regulatory standards such as GDPR for data protection or HIPAA for healthcare information. Understanding these standards is not just about passing the exam; it's about being prepared for the professional challenges you'll face in the field.
Let's talk more on these below;

Basic Security Concepts

Security isn't just a technical requirement but a critical line of defense against a broad range of threats that organizations face daily.

Let's begin with the concept of "threats," the underlying reason why security measures exist. In the realm of networking, threats can be both external and internal. External threats often make headlines—cybercriminals, hackers, and nation-state actors attempting to compromise systems. However, internal threats—disgruntled employees, accidental data deletion, or even uninformed staff clicking on phishing links—are equally dangerous. The point is, understanding the variety of threats helps you tailor your security measures more effectively.

The next cornerstone in our journey through basic security concepts is "vulnerability." Imagine a fortress; its strength isn't just in its armed guards but also in identifying and reinforcing any weak walls or broken gates. In the digital realm, a vulnerability is akin to these weak walls—a software bug, a misconfigured server, or even a forgotten open port can serve as a point of entry for attackers. Understanding vulnerabilities is essential, as it is through these gaps that threats often become attacks.

Now, let's talk about something called the "AAA framework," which stands for Authentication, Authorization, and Accounting. This is a model used to control user access and monitor activity within a network.

Authentication is the process of verifying the identity of a person or system. This is usually the first step in any secure communication.

Authorization involves permissions and restrictions—basically what authenticated users are allowed or not allowed to do.

Accounting keeps track of what the authenticated user does during a session, creating an audit trail that can be used for various kinds of analysis later.

While the AAA framework helps ensure only authorized personnel have access, it's equally crucial to have a robust "firewall" in place. Firewalls act as gatekeepers, controlling incoming and outgoing network traffic based on an organization's previously established security policies. They're a primary defense against unauthorized access and can be either hardware or software-based.

In addition to firewalls, "Intrusion Detection Systems (IDS)" and "Intrusion Prevention Systems (IPS)" play a pivotal role. These systems monitor network traffic for suspicious activity. While IDS is like a vigilant watchdog that barks at intruders, IPS takes it a step further by also blocking potential threats.

And lastly "encryption." In simplest terms, encryption is the process of converting readable data into an unreadable format to protect its confidentiality. While encryption doesn't prevent intrusion, it does ensure that even if data is intercepted, it would be unreadable to the unauthorized individual.

Firewalls and IDS/IPS Systems

A key component of network security involves implementing firewalls and Intrusion Detection Systems (IDS) / Intrusion Prevention Systems (IPS). These tools are critical in identifying and blocking malicious traffic, and thereby safeguarding the network from unauthorized access and cyberattacks.

Understanding Firewalls

A firewall acts as a barrier between a trusted network, such as a corporate local area network (LAN), and an untrusted network, like the internet. It monitors incoming and outgoing traffic and decides whether to allow or block specific data packets based on a set of security rules or policies.

Firewalls can be hardware devices, software applications, or a combination of both. Hardware firewalls are standalone devices positioned between a computer (or a network) and the external network (or internet). They are usually more robust and can handle more traffic, making them suitable for large organizations. Software firewalls, on the other hand, are installed on individual computers or servers. They are easier to customize but might impact the system's performance as they use its resources.

There are different types of firewalls, each working at different layers of the OSI model and providing varying levels of security:

Packet-Filtering Firewalls: These operate at the network layer (Layer 3) and make decisions based on the source and destination IP addresses, ports, and protocols.

Stateful Inspection Firewalls: Operating at the network layer as well, these firewalls keep track of the state of active connections and make decisions based on the context of the traffic.

Proxy Firewalls: These operate at the application layer (Layer 7) and act as intermediaries between the client and the server, filtering traffic at the application level.

Next-Generation Firewalls (NGFW): These are advanced firewalls that combine traditional firewall capabilities with other network security functions like intrusion prevention and application control.

Understanding IDS and IPS
Intrusion Detection Systems (IDS) and Intrusion Prevention Systems (IPS) are crucial components of network security that monitor network traffic for signs of malicious activity or security policy violations.

Intrusion Detection Systems (IDS): An IDS monitors network traffic and alerts administrators when it detects suspicious activity or anomalies. It does not take any action to block the traffic; instead, it relies on the administrators to analyze the alerts and take appropriate actions. There are two main types of IDS:

Network-based IDS (NIDS): Monitors traffic across the entire network or a specific segment.

Host-based IDS (HIDS): Monitors traffic on a specific host or device.

Intrusion Prevention Systems (IPS): An IPS is similar to an IDS, but it takes it a step further by automatically taking action to block the suspicious traffic. Like IDS, IPS can also be network-based (NIPS) or host-based (HIPS).

Configuring and Managing Firewalls and IDS/IPS

Properly configuring and managing firewalls and IDS/IPS is crucial for optimal network security. Here are some best practices:

Define Security Policies: Clearly define the security policies and rules that the firewall and IDS/IPS will enforce. These policies should be aligned with the organization's security requirements and compliance standards.

Regularly Update Signatures: IDS/IPS systems rely on signatures or patterns of known attacks to identify malicious traffic. Regularly update these signatures to ensure the systems can detect the latest threats.

Implement Least Privilege Principle: Configure the firewall to deny all traffic by default and only allow necessary traffic. This minimizes the attack surface.

Monitor and Analyze Logs: Regularly monitor and analyze the logs generated by the firewall and IDS/IPS to identify any suspicious activities or security incidents.

Firewalls and IDS/IPS systems are essential tools for securing a network and protecting it from cyber threats. Understanding how they work, their different types, and how to configure and manage them properly is crucial for anyone aspiring to become a network security professional.

VPNs and Remote Access

Virtual Private Networks (VPNs) and remote access technologies facilitate secure communication and access to resources over the internet.

Virtual Private Networks (VPNs)

VPNs are a crucial technology that enables secure communication over an untrusted network, such as the internet. A VPN creates a private tunnel over the public network, ensuring that the data transmitted is encrypted and secure from unauthorized access.

- VPN Components: The essential components of a VPN include the VPN client, VPN server, and the VPN gateway. The client is the device that initiates the VPN connection, usually a computer or mobile device. The server is the device that the client connects to, and the gateway is the device that manages the traffic between the client and the server.
- Types of VPNs: There are two main types of VPNs, Site-to-Site VPNs and Remote Access VPNs. Site-to-Site VPNs connect entire networks to each other, for example, connecting a branch office network to a company's headquarters network. Remote Access VPNs, on the other hand, connect individual devices to a network, such as an employee connecting to the company's network from home.
- VPN Protocols: Several protocols are used to establish and secure VPN connections. Some of the most common ones include IPsec (Internet Protocol Security), PPTP (Point-to-Point Tunneling Protocol), and L2TP (Layer 2 Tunneling Protocol).

Remote Access

Remote access technologies enable users to access resources on a network from a remote location. This capability is particularly important for businesses with a distributed workforce or for employees who need to access network resources while traveling.

- Remote Desktop: This is a technology that allows a user to control a computer from a remote location, as if they were sitting directly in front of it. Tools like Microsoft's Remote Desktop Protocol (RDP) and third-party applications like TeamViewer facilitate remote desktop access.
- Virtual Network Computing (VNC): VNC is another remote desktop access tool that uses the RFB (Remote Framebuffer) protocol to control another computer remotely.
- Secure Shell (SSH): This is a cryptographic network protocol that enables secure remote login and other secure network services over an insecure network.

Security Considerations

Ensuring the security of data transmission is paramount when utilizing VPNs and remote access technologies.

- Encryption: Encrypting the data before transmission is crucial to maintaining its confidentiality. Most VPNs use strong encryption algorithms to ensure data security.
- Authentication: This involves verifying the identity of the devices or users attempting to establish a VPN or remote access connection. It is crucial to ensure that only authorized users can access the network resources.
- Authorization: Once a user is authenticated, they must be authorized to access specific resources on the network. This ensures that users only have access to the resources necessary for their role.

VPNs and remote access technologies are essential tools for modern businesses and IT professionals. They facilitate secure communication and access to resources over the internet, enabling distributed workforces to collaborate effectively and securely.

Wireless Security

Wireless networks have become ubiquitous in today's world, providing the convenience of accessing the internet and network resources without being tethered by cables. However, this convenience comes with its own set of security challenges. This section aims to provide a comprehensive understanding of the various aspects of wireless security, from understanding the potential threats to implementing security measures to protect a wireless network.

Potential Threats to Wireless Networks
Understanding the potential threats to wireless networks is the first step towards securing them. Unlike wired networks, wireless networks use radio waves to transmit data, making it possible for attackers to intercept the data or gain unauthorized access to the network.

Eavesdropping: This is the act of intercepting and listening to the communication on a wireless network without authorization. Attackers can use special tools to capture the data packets transmitted over the network and extract sensitive information.

Unauthorized Access: Attackers can gain unauthorized access to a wireless network by cracking the network's security key or exploiting vulnerabilities in the network's security configuration.

Man-in-the-Middle Attacks: In this type of attack, an attacker intercepts the communication between two parties on the network, potentially altering the data before it reaches its intended destination.

Denial of Service (DoS) Attacks: Attackers can overwhelm a wireless network with excessive traffic, causing the network to become slow or unavailable for legitimate users.

Securing Wireless Networks
Securing a wireless network involves implementing various security measures to protect the network from unauthorized access and data breaches.

Use Strong Encryption: Encryption is the process of converting data into a coded form to prevent unauthorized access. Using strong encryption algorithms, such as WPA3 (Wi-Fi Protected Access 3), is essential for securing the data transmitted over a wireless network.

Implement MAC Address Filtering: Each wireless device has a unique MAC (Media Access Control) address. By implementing MAC address filtering, you can restrict access to the network to only those devices with MAC addresses listed in the allowed list.

Use Strong Passwords: Implementing strong, unique passwords for accessing the wireless network and administrative interfaces is crucial for preventing unauthorized access.

Disable SSID Broadcasting: The SSID (Service Set Identifier) is the name of a wireless network. By disabling SSID broadcasting, the network will not be visible to devices scanning for available networks, making it less likely for attackers to target the network.

Implement a Wireless Intrusion Prevention System (WIPS): A WIPS monitors the wireless network for any unusual activities or attacks and takes appropriate actions to prevent unauthorized access or data breaches.

Regularly Update Firmware and Software: Keeping the firmware and software of wireless devices updated is essential for fixing any known vulnerabilities and improving the security of the network.

Segregate the Network: Creating separate networks for guests and internal users can help minimize the risk of unauthorized access to sensitive network resources.

Understanding the potential threats to wireless networks and implementing the appropriate security measures is crucial for protecting the network from unauthorized access and data breaches. By implementing strong encryption, using strong passwords, implementing MAC address filtering, disabling SSID broadcasting, and regularly updating firmware and software, you can significantly improve the security of your wireless network. Additionally, implementing a WIPS and segregating the network can provide additional layers of security.

Security Policies and Compliance

Security is not a static concept, but a dynamic ongoing process. While hardware and software measures like firewalls and IDS/IPS systems are essential, they are but half of the equation. The other half resides in the establishment and enforcement of robust security policies, as well as ensuring compliance with both internal and external standards. As you navigate the path to earning your CompTIA Network+ certification, it is crucial to grasp the import of these non-technical elements in the overarching network security landscape.

Let's delve into security policies first. These are essentially the rulebooks that govern how an organization's network—along with its associated hardware, software, and human components—should operate to maintain security. While it's tempting to think of a security policy as a one-size-fits-all document, the reality is far more nuanced. Each organization will have unique needs based on its size, industry, and the nature of the data it handles. For instance, a healthcare organization would need stringent policies to protect sensitive patient data, often guided by regulations such as HIPAA. On the other hand, a tech startup might be more focused on intellectual property protection and would thus tailor its policies accordingly.

Now, while creating a security policy, several key areas require careful consideration:

- **Access Control**: This stipulates who has permission to access which resources. It's not just about preventing unauthorized access but also about ensuring authorized personnel have the level of access they need—and no more.
- **Data Protection**: This entails how data is encrypted, stored, and transmitted. It is particularly essential in organizations that handle sensitive information.
- **Incident Response Plan**: This is the game plan for how to handle potential security incidents. This plan should be so thorough that even in the heat of a crisis, anyone can pick it up and know exactly what steps to take.
- **Regular Audits and Monitoring**: This involves tracking how well the network is secured and if the policy measures are effective.

The second part of this part focuses on compliance, another cornerstone in the architecture of network security. While security policies are often internally focused, compliance brings in an external perspective. It's not just about what your organization thinks is best but also about aligning your network security practices with external regulations and standards. For example, if your company operates within the European Union, compliance with the General Data Protection Regulation (GDPR) isn't optional—it's a legal requirement.

Compliance isn't a "set it and forget it" undertaking but an ongoing process. It involves regular audits, both internal and external, to ensure your network meets or exceeds the necessary standards. Sometimes these audits can expose gaps in your security posture, providing a valuable opportunity for improvement. More importantly, failing to maintain compliance can result in severe penalties, both financial and reputational.

In preparation for your CompTIA Network+ exam, understanding the relationship between security policies and compliance is not just textbook knowledge. It's practical, real-world information that you'll use throughout your career. You'll likely find yourself in situations where you'll have to draft or revise security policies or ensure that your network is compliant with newly enacted laws or regulations.

Chapter 6: Troubleshooting

When you're in the field of networking, the reality is that things won't always go according to plan. Servers go down, connections get lost, and performance can fluctuate. Troubleshooting is not just a skill but an art form, built on a combination of technical knowledge, logical reasoning, and a dash of intuition. In this chapter, we delve deep into the realm of troubleshooting and explore the methodologies used to diagnose issues, tools that can assist you, and some of the most common challenges you may encounter.

Troubleshooting Methodology

Troubleshooting is often considered an art form, layered on a foundation of technical skills and a deep understanding of networking concepts. While technology and tools can assist in the process, it's your methodology that will set you apart.

The Importance of Methodology

Understanding the *why* behind troubleshooting is just as critical as the *how*. A well-defined methodology not only makes you efficient but also ensures that you solve problems in a way that is logical and repeatable. It serves as your road map, particularly when you are confronted with complex issues where the root cause is not immediately evident. The methodology allows you to take a step back, evaluate the situation, and then dive into problem-solving with a clear direction. In this way, you not only solve the immediate issue at hand but also gain insights that could be valuable for preventing similar issues in the future.

The first step in establishing an effective troubleshooting methodology is adopting a structured approach. In networking, problems can arise from a variety of sources—hardware, software, user error, or even external factors like security threats. A structured approach ensures that you proceed in a logical and organized manner, helping you to identify the root cause efficiently.

The general workflow involves:

1. **Identification**: Recognize the problem, understand its scope, and confirm that it actually exists.

2. **Isolation**: Narrow down the source of the issue, whether it's localized to a specific system or affecting a broader network segment.

3. **Diagnosis**: Utilize diagnostic tools and your understanding of networking principles to identify the root cause.

4. **Resolution and Verification**: Implement the solution and verify that it has resolved the issue.

5. **Documentation**: Record the problem, the steps taken to resolve it, and any lessons learned for future reference.

Diagnostic Tools: The Troubleshooter's Arsenal

Having the right tools at your disposal can dramatically speed up the troubleshooting process. Network analyzers, packet sniffers, and various software utilities are not just instruments but extensions of your skills. However, keep in mind that tools are only as effective as the person using them. Knowing when to employ a particular tool is just as crucial as understanding its functionality. A seasoned network professional is often distinguished not by the complexity of the tools they use but by the mastery of basic utilities to diagnose complex issues effectively.

Applying Logic and Intuition

You might be wondering, "Where does intuition come into play in a field so technical?" The answer is—quite a lot. With experience, you'll start to see patterns in how certain issues manifest. Sometimes, your gut feeling will guide you towards a quick resolution. However, it's essential that intuition never replaces a structured approach but rather complements it. When you're troubleshooting under pressure, a balance of logic and intuition can often lead to faster and more effective solutions.

The Role of Communication

Troubleshooting is rarely a solitary endeavor. Whether you're in a team setting or interfacing with end-users experiencing the problems, communication skills are crucial. Effective communication ensures that you get all the necessary information to identify and resolve issues. It also helps in creating a collaborative environment where ideas can be exchanged freely, providing different perspectives that might prove invaluable in solving more complex problems.

Closing Thoughts

Troubleshooting can be a rewarding experience, especially when you can resolve issues that have a tangible impact on your organization's performance or security. By adopting a robust troubleshooting methodology, you not only equip yourself with a systematic approach to solving problems but also develop a mindset that prepares you for the inevitable challenges in your networking career.

Identifying Network Problems

Despite the best planning and implementation, issues will arise that need to be addressed promptly and efficiently. The ability to identify network problems quickly and accurately is a critical skill for any network professional. Here, we will focus on the various types of network problems that may arise, the tools and techniques that can be used to identify them, and the steps that can be taken to resolve them.

Common Network Problems

First, let us delve into some common network problems that you may encounter:

1. **Slow Performance:** This is often the first sign that there is a problem with the network. Slow performance can be caused by a variety of factors, including high network traffic, faulty network devices, or even external attacks like Distributed Denial of Service (DDoS) attacks.

2. **Intermittent Connectivity:** This refers to a network connection that is unstable or sporadically available. It can be caused by physical interference, faulty hardware, or configuration errors.

3. **Complete Network Outage:** This is the most severe network problem, where the entire network or a significant portion of it becomes unavailable. This can be caused by catastrophic hardware failure, severe external attacks, or major configuration errors.

4. **Security Breaches:** Unauthorized access to the network or its resources is a critical problem that can lead to data loss, data theft, or even complete network compromise.

5. **Inconsistent Behavior:** This refers to network devices or applications behaving erratically or differently than expected. This can be caused by software bugs, hardware malfunctions, or configuration errors.

Steps to Identify Network Problems

Identifying network problems involves a series of steps that should be followed systematically:

1. **Identify the Symptoms:** The first step in identifying a network problem is to recognize the symptoms. This may involve interviewing users, monitoring network traffic, or using network management tools to gather information about the current state of the network.

2. **Isolate the Problem:** Once you have identified the symptoms, the next step is to isolate the problem to a specific network segment, device, or application. This may involve reviewing network documentation, analyzing network traffic, or performing tests to identify the exact location of the problem.

3. **Analyze the Data:** After isolating the problem, you need to analyze the data collected to identify the root cause of the problem. This may involve reviewing logs, analyzing packet captures, or consulting vendor documentation.

4. **Formulate a Hypothesis:** Based on the data collected and analyzed, you should formulate a hypothesis about the root cause of the problem. This hypothesis should be tested to confirm its accuracy before proceeding to the next step.

5. **Test the Hypothesis:** Test the hypothesis by making controlled changes to the network configuration, hardware, or software, and observe the effects. If the problem is resolved, you can conclude that your hypothesis was correct. If not, you may need to revise your hypothesis and repeat the testing process.

6. **Document the Findings:** Finally, it is crucial to document your findings, including the symptoms observed, the steps taken to isolate and identify the problem, the hypothesis formulated, the tests conducted, and the final resolution. This documentation will be helpful in resolving similar problems in the future and for maintaining a record of network issues and resolutions.

Identifying network problems is a critical skill for network professionals and is a key component of the CompTIA Network+ certification exam. By following a systematic approach to problem identification and resolution, you can quickly and accurately identify and resolve network problems, minimizing downtime and ensuring the smooth operation of the network. Remember to document your findings thoroughly, as this will be valuable for future troubleshooting and for maintaining a record of network issues and resolutions

Tools for Troubleshooting

Troubleshooting is akin to detective work: you're presented with a situation, often with limited information, and your task is to unearth the truth—what is causing the issue? It's a dynamic interplay of knowledge, intuition, and the right set of tools.

Protocol Analyzers

One of the linchpins in troubleshooting tools is the protocol analyzer, commonly known as a packet sniffer. This software captures data packets that traverse the network, allowing for real-time or retrospective analysis. Whether you're trying to pinpoint the cause of intermittent network slow-downs or inspect the data packets for security breaches, a protocol analyzer provides an in-depth look into the network's traffic. Tools like Wireshark are often the go-to choice for many network administrators. They enable professionals to dissect data packets layer by layer, from the application right down to the physical layer, aiding in the detection of anomalies that could be the root cause of network issues.

Command Line Utilities

For many network professionals, command-line utilities are the bread and butter of troubleshooting tools. They offer a quick and resource-light means of scanning network configurations and statuses. Commands like **ping** to test connectivity,

tracert to map network paths, and **netstat** to view network statistics are used ubiquitously in the troubleshooting process.

The charm of command-line utilities is their availability; they're often built into operating systems and require no additional software installation. They allow network administrators to rapidly diagnose problems by simply inputting specific commands, receiving instant feedback that helps identify issues such as packet loss or routing errors.

Remote Desktop Tools

Imagine being able to sit at your desk and resolve a network issue halfway across the world. Remote desktop tools make this a reality. They allow network administrators to connect to a remote computer as if they were sitting right in front of it, offering a vital lifeline for troubleshooting issues that arise in distant locations. Platforms like TeamViewer or Remote Desktop Protocol (RDP) for Windows environments are vital in modern network management. These tools often come with additional features like file transfer capabilities, multi-monitor support, and even session recording, providing an extensive utility set for diagnosing and resolving issues remotely.

Hardware Tools

While software tools often take the spotlight, hardware tools are indispensable in specific scenarios, especially when you're troubleshooting issues at the physical layer of the network. A cable tester, for instance, can save hours of guesswork by quickly determining whether a connectivity issue is due to a faulty Ethernet cable. Similarly, a network multimeter can measure various network parameters like voltage and current, aiding in the diagnosis of hardware malfunctions.

Monitoring Software

Last but certainly not least is network monitoring software. Think of it as the radar system of your network operations center. Tools like Nagios or SolarWinds provide a dashboard view of your network's health, tracking performance metrics and alerting administrators to issues before they become critical. They monitor various aspects like bandwidth usage, server performance, and even environmental variables like temperature in server rooms, providing a holistic view of the network's wellbeing.

In dealing with network troubleshooting, the right tool for the job might vary depending on the problem at hand. From protocol analyzers to simple command-line utilities, from remote desktop platforms to tangible hardware tools, and from comprehensive monitoring software to specialized utilities, each has a specific role in the larger puzzle of network health. It's up to the network professional to master these tools, understanding their nuances and capabilities, to effectively diagnose and resolve network issues.

Troubleshooting Common Issues (Connectivity, Performance, etc.)

There are several common issues that can arise in a network, including connectivity problems, performance issues, and other common challenges.

Connectivity Issues

Connectivity issues are perhaps the most common type of network problem. These can occur for various reasons, from incorrect configurations to faulty hardware. When troubleshooting connectivity issues, it's essential to approach the problem systematically. Start by checking the physical layer to ensure that all cables and connectors are secure and functioning correctly. Next, check the data link layer to ensure that the switches and MAC addresses are correctly configured. Moving up the layers, check the network layer to ensure that IP addresses, subnets, and routing are all correctly configured. Finally, check the transport and application layers to ensure that the necessary ports are open and that the application is correctly configured.

Some common connectivity issues include:

- **IP Address Conflicts**: When two devices on the same network are assigned the same IP address, it results in an IP address conflict. This can cause intermittent connectivity or complete loss of connection for the affected devices. To resolve this issue, check the DHCP server to ensure that the IP address range is correctly configured and that there are no static IP addresses that conflict with the DHCP range.

- **Subnet Mask Mismatch**: A subnet mask mismatch occurs when two devices on the same network are configured with different subnet masks. This can result in the devices being unable to communicate with each other, even though they are on the same network. To resolve this issue, ensure that all devices on the network are configured with the correct subnet mask.

- **Default Gateway Misconfiguration**: The default gateway is the IP address of the router that a device uses to access networks outside its local subnet. If the default gateway is incorrectly configured, a device may be unable to access the internet or other networks outside its local subnet. To resolve this issue, ensure that the default gateway is correctly configured on all devices and routers on the network.

Performance Issues

Performance issues can manifest in various ways, from slow data transfer speeds to intermittent connectivity. These issues can be caused by a variety of factors, such as network congestion, faulty hardware, or incorrect configurations.

Some common performance issues include:

- **Network Congestion**: Network congestion occurs when there is too much traffic on a network, resulting in slow data transfer speeds and packet loss. This can be caused by too many devices connected to the network, large file transfers, or high bandwidth applications like video streaming. To resolve network congestion, consider implementing Quality of Service (QoS) settings on your routers and switches to prioritize traffic, upgrading your network infrastructure to support higher bandwidth, or segmenting your network to reduce congestion.

- **Packet Loss**: Packet loss occurs when data packets sent from one device to another are lost during transmission. This can result in slow data transfer speeds, choppy audio or video, and intermittent connectivity. Packet loss can be caused by network congestion, faulty hardware, or incorrect configurations. To troubleshoot packet loss, use a tool like ping or traceroute to identify where the packets are being lost, and then check the devices along that path for any issues.

- **Bandwidth Limitations**: Bandwidth limitations occur when the available bandwidth on a network is insufficient to handle the amount of traffic being generated. This can result in slow data transfer speeds and intermittent connectivity. To resolve bandwidth limitations, consider upgrading your network infrastructure to support higher bandwidth, implementing QoS settings to prioritize traffic, or segmenting your network to reduce congestion.

Other Common Issues

In addition to connectivity and performance issues, there are several other common problems that you may encounter in a network:

- **DNS Issues**: DNS issues occur when a device is unable to resolve domain names to IP addresses. This can result in a device being unable to access websites or other resources on the internet. To troubleshoot DNS issues, check the DNS server settings on the affected device and ensure that they are correctly configured. Additionally, check the DNS server itself to ensure that it is functioning correctly and that it has the correct entries for the domain names in question.

- **DHCP Issues**: DHCP issues occur when a device is unable to obtain an IP address from a DHCP server. This can result in the device being unable to connect to the network. To troubleshoot DHCP issues, check the DHCP server settings to ensure that it is correctly configured and that there are enough available IP addresses in the DHCP range. Additionally, check the affected device to ensure that it is configured to obtain an IP address automatically.

- **Router and Switch Configuration**: Incorrect configurations on routers and switches can result in a variety of network issues. For example, incorrect VLAN configurations can result in devices being unable to communicate with each other, and incorrect routing configurations can result in devices being unable to access the internet or other networks. To troubleshoot router and switch configuration issues, check the configurations on the affected devices and ensure that they are correctly configured for your network.

Troubleshooting network issues can be a daunting task, but by approaching the problem systematically and understanding the common issues that can occur, you can quickly identify and resolve the problem. Remember to start at the physical layer and work your way up, checking each layer for potential issues. Additionally, having a strong understanding of networking concepts and configurations will greatly aid in your troubleshooting efforts. By mastering the skills covered in this chapter, you will be well-equipped to troubleshoot common network issues and ensure the smooth operation of your network.

Chapter 7: Industry Standards, Practices, and Network Theory

Standards are pivotal in any industry, but they take on particular importance in the field of networking. Industry standards enable interoperability, promote security, and facilitate communication among different devices and systems. They are established by various organizations, such as the Institute of Electrical and Electronics Engineers (IEEE), the American National Standards Institute (ANSI), and the International Organization for Standardization (ISO), to name a few.

- **IEEE Standards**: For example, IEEE 802.11 governs wireless networking. Knowing this standard helps you understand how to set up, manage, and troubleshoot wireless networks.

- **ANSI Standards**: The ANSI X3.92 standard, for instance, pertains to data encryption. This standard ensures that encryption across networks is consistent, thereby ensuring data integrity and security.

- **ISO Standards**: The ISO 27001 focuses on information security management systems. Being familiar with this can help you understand the broad strokes of setting up secure network operations.

By aligning with these standards, you demonstrate to stakeholders that you are committed to quality, performance, and security. Moreover, adhering to industry standards can often be a legal requirement, especially when dealing with sensitive information.

A thorough grounding in industry standards, best practices, and network theory not only amplifies your technical skills but also situates you within the broader ecosystem of network professionals. Understanding this dimension of networking ensures that you are not merely a technician but a professional capable of strategic decision-making. As such, this chapter is your gateway to understanding the foundational frameworks and guidelines that govern the industry.

Best Practices

Adhering to best practices ensures the optimization of network performance, enhances security, and facilitates the management and growth of the network.

Importance of Best Practices

Best practices in networking are more than just guidelines; they represent collective experience distilled into actionable steps. Adhering to best practices not only optimizes network performance but also mitigates risks and streamlines management. This is crucial because a well-configured network is often the differentiating factor between an efficient, secure organization and one plagued by outages, security breaches, and inefficiencies.

Documentation

The first step in establishing best practices is robust documentation. While it may seem tedious, the importance of comprehensive documentation cannot be overstated. A well-documented network serves as a roadmap for network management, troubleshooting, and future planning. This includes network diagrams, configurations, hardware and software inventories, and even logs of changes and updates. When you have a record to refer to, identifying the root cause of issues or planning upgrades becomes exponentially easier.

Change Management

Implementing an effective change management process is another key aspect of network best practices. Change management is the systematic approach to handling alterations to the network configuration or hardware to minimize risk and interruptions. This involves planning, testing, and documenting changes, along with a rollback plan in case things don't go as expected.

Security Protocols

Security is an ever-present concern in today's network landscape. Therefore, integrating security best practices into your routine is essential. This involves multifaceted strategies like ensuring all default passwords are changed, implementing firewalls and intrusion detection systems, and regular patch management. Being proactive about security, rather than reactive, can prevent a host of issues down the line, making it a cornerstone of any set of best practices.

Redundancy and Failover Strategies

When we talk about best practices, the concept of redundancy is often front and center. In essence, redundancy is about having backup systems or methods in place to take over if your primary systems fail. Whether it's an extra server, backup power supply, or even an alternative data route, these redundancies can save a lot of time, money, and stress when things go wrong. Coupled with this is the failover strategy, a predefined set of procedures that dictates how your network will respond to different types of failures.

Regular Audits and Reviews

Conducting regular audits and reviews of your network can reveal inefficiencies and vulnerabilities that might otherwise go unnoticed. This allows for proactive management of potential issues and an opportunity to optimize network performance. Regular checks on hardware health, software updates, and even things as simple as cable management can make a significant difference in the long run.

End-User Training

Lastly, it's important to consider the human element in any network. Even the most robust, well-configured system can be vulnerable if end-users are not educated about potential risks and best practices. Training programs on the responsible use of network resources, recognizing phishing attempts, and maintaining strong passwords can go a long way in safeguarding your network.

Mastering these best practices is not merely a preparatory step for your CompTIA Network+ certification. It's a lifelong skill that will serve you well in your professional career, ensuring that you not only understand the technical aspects of networking but also appreciate the nuances that come with maintaining a secure, efficient, and reliable network.

Policies and Procedures

In networking, much like other disciplines within the IT sector, is governed by a series of policies and procedures designed to ensure consistency, security, and efficiency in the management and operation of networks. Understanding these policies and procedures is not only essential for the CompTIA Network+ exam but also crucial for your success as a network professional. This part aims to provide an in-depth analysis of the key policies and procedures that every aspiring network professional should be familiar with.

Network Policy

A network policy is a set of rules and guidelines that dictate how a network should be managed and used. It covers a wide range of areas including, but not limited to, access control, usage, security, and management. A well-defined network policy is essential for maintaining the integrity, availability, and confidentiality of network resources.

Access Control Policy

Access control policies define who or what can access network resources and to what extent. These policies are crucial for safeguarding sensitive data and preventing unauthorized access. They typically involve the implementation of user accounts, passwords, and permissions. Moreover, access control policies also dictate the use of authentication methods such as username/password, digital certificates, or multi-factor authentication.

Usage Policy

A network usage policy outlines the acceptable use of the network by its users. This includes guidelines on internet usage, email usage, social media, and the use of personal devices on the network. For instance, a network usage policy may prohibit the use of peer-to-peer file sharing applications or the access to certain websites. It is essential that all users are aware of and understand the network usage policy to prevent misuse and ensure network security.

Security Policy

Security policies form the backbone of network security. They encompass a variety of rules and guidelines designed to protect the network from threats, both internal and external. This includes policies on firewall configuration, intrusion detection and prevention systems (IDS/IPS), virtual private networks (VPNs), and encryption.

A well-crafted security policy is essential for safeguarding the network and its resources from unauthorized access, data breaches, and cyberattacks.

Management Policy

Management policies are designed to ensure the efficient and effective operation of the network. These policies often involve guidelines on network monitoring, configuration management, backup and recovery, and software updates. For instance, a management policy may dictate that all network devices must be configured according to a standard template and that configuration changes must be documented and approved by a network administrator.

Compliance Requirements

In addition to internal policies and procedures, network professionals must also be aware of external compliance requirements that may apply to their organization. These may include legal and regulatory requirements such as the General Data Protection Regulation (GDPR) or the Health Insurance Portability and Accountability Act (HIPAA). Compliance with these requirements is mandatory and failure to do so may result in legal penalties and reputational damage.

Documentation

Documentation is a critical aspect of network management and is often required by both internal policies and external compliance requirements. Proper documentation ensures that the network can be managed effectively, facilitates troubleshooting, and provides a record of network changes and incidents. Documentation may include network diagrams, configuration files, incident reports, and change request forms.

Conclusion

Understanding and adhering to network policies and procedures is essential for the effective management and operation of networks. It ensures consistency, security, and efficiency, and is a key component of the CompTIA Network+ exam. By mastering the concepts outlined in this chapter, you will be well-equipped to manage and secure networks in a professional environment and well on your way to acing the exam

Industry Standards (IEEE, ANSI, etc.)

Behind the scenes, governing bodies and organizations work diligently to create and maintain industry standards that ensure interoperability, reliability, and quality across various network technologies. The importance of these standards cannot be overstated, especially when you consider the diverse range of devices and technologies that need to communicate with each other in a modern network.

The Importance of Industry Standards

Industry standards are a set of criteria, specifications, and guidelines established by recognized organizations in the IT industry. These standards are developed collaboratively by experts, industry stakeholders, and sometimes even competitors, with the aim of ensuring that products and services are consistent, compatible, and efficient across the board.

- **Interoperability**: This is perhaps the most significant advantage of industry standards. They ensure that products from different vendors can work together seamlessly. This is crucial in a world where a network might comprise devices and services from multiple vendors.

- **Reliability**: Standards ensure that products and services meet a certain level of quality and performance. This is essential for building and maintaining reliable networks.

- **Innovation**: Industry standards provide a platform for innovation. They offer a common ground for inventors and innovators to build upon, ensuring that new products and services are compatible with existing ones.

- **Economic Benefits**: Standards contribute to the economy by enabling mass production of devices and services, reducing costs, and facilitating international trade.

Key Organizations and Their Roles

Several organizations are involved in the development and maintenance of industry standards. Here are a few key players:

- **IEEE (Institute of Electrical and Electronics Engineers)**: This is one of the most influential organizations in the IT industry. It develops standards for a wide range of technologies, including networking, telecommunications, and computing.

- **IETF (Internet Engineering Task Force)**: This organization is responsible for developing and promoting voluntary Internet standards, particularly the standards that comprise the Internet protocol suite (TCP/IP).

- **ISO (International Organization for Standardization)**: This is a global organization that develops and publishes international standards for various industries, including IT.

- **ANSI (American National Standards Institute)**: This organization oversees the development of standards in the United States, including those related to IT and networking.

Standards in Networking

In the context of networking, there are several key standards that any networking professional should be familiar with. Here are a few examples:

- **Ethernet (IEEE 802.3)**: This is the most widely used local area networking (LAN) technology. It defines the physical and data link layers of the OSI model.

- **Wi-Fi (IEEE 802.11)**: This standard defines the technology for wireless LANs. It covers the physical and data link layers of the OSI model.

- **IP (Internet Protocol, RFC 791)**: This is the principal communications protocol in the Internet protocol suite for relaying datagrams across network boundaries.

- **TCP (Transmission Control Protocol, RFC 793)**: This is one of the main protocols in the Internet protocol suite. It is responsible for ensuring the reliable transmission of data across a network.

Compliance Requirements

In addition to the technical standards, there are also compliance requirements that networks need to adhere to. These are often related to data protection, privacy, and security. For example:

- **GDPR (General Data Protection Regulation)**: This is a regulation in EU law on data protection and privacy in the European Union and the European Economic Area. It also addresses the transfer of personal data outside these regions.

- **HIPAA (Health Insurance Portability and Accountability Act)**: This is a US law designed to provide privacy standards to protect patients' medical records and other health information.

Industry standards play a crucial role in the world of networking. They ensure interoperability, reliability, and innovation, and they have significant economic benefits. Key organizations like the IEEE, IETF, ISO, and ANSI are responsible for developing and maintaining these standards. Networking professionals must be familiar with key networking standards like Ethernet, Wi-Fi, IP, and TCP, as well as compliance requirements like GDPR and HIPAA. A thorough understanding of these standards is essential for success in the CompTIA Network+ exam and a fruitful career in networking.

Compliance Requirements (HIPAA, GDPR, etc.)

Based on our subject matter, compliance refers to the process of ensuring that an organization's IT systems, operations, and data are managed in accordance with established laws, regulations, and standards. It is an essential aspect of network management that is often overlooked by professionals focused on the technical aspects of their roles. Compliance is not just a legal requirement but also a critical component of an organization's risk management strategy. As a network professional, you will likely be involved in ensuring that your organization's network is compliant with various regulations, standards, and best practices.

Understanding the Different Types of Compliance

There are several types of compliance requirements that an organization may need to adhere to, depending on its location, industry, and the nature of the data it handles. These can be broadly categorized into three types:

1. Legal and Regulatory Compliance: These are the laws and regulations imposed by government bodies. Examples include the General Data Protection Regulation (GDPR) in the European Union, which governs the

handling of personal data, and the Health Insurance Portability and Accountability Act (HIPAA) in the United States, which regulates the use and disclosure of protected health information.

2. Industry-specific Compliance: These are standards and regulations specific to a particular industry. For example, the Payment Card Industry Data Security Standard (PCI DSS) is a set of security standards designed to ensure that all companies that accept, process, store, or transmit credit card information maintain a secure environment.

3. Organizational Compliance: These are the policies, procedures, and standards established by an organization to govern its operations and ensure the security and integrity of its data. These may be developed internally or adopted from industry best practices and standards.

Ensuring compliance in network operations involves several key steps:

1. Understanding the Requirements: The first step in ensuring compliance is to understand the specific requirements that apply to your organization. This involves a thorough analysis of all relevant laws, regulations, and standards, and understanding how they apply to your organization's network operations.

2. Conducting a Gap Analysis: Once you understand the requirements, you need to assess your organization's current network operations to identify any gaps in compliance. This involves reviewing your existing policies, procedures, and controls to determine if they meet the required standards.

3. Implementing Necessary Changes: After identifying the gaps, you need to develop and implement a plan to address them. This may involve updating policies and procedures, implementing new controls, or making changes to the network architecture.

4. Regular Monitoring and Auditing: Compliance is not a one-time activity but an ongoing process. Regular monitoring and auditing of network operations are necessary to ensure continued compliance with all relevant requirements.

5. Documentation: Proper documentation of all policies, procedures, and controls is essential for demonstrating compliance to auditors and regulatory bodies. This includes maintaining records of all assessments, changes implemented, and monitoring activities.

Preparing for the CompTIA Network+ Exam

The CompTIA Network+ exam assesses your knowledge and skills in various areas of network operations, including compliance. You will be expected to demonstrate an understanding of common practices for network configuration and management, as well as the implications of different laws, standards, and policies on network operations. To prepare for the exam, it is important to familiarize yourself with the key concepts of compliance as they relate to network operations and to understand the steps involved in ensuring compliance in an organization.

Lastly, compliance is a critical aspect of network operations that every network professional should understand. It involves understanding the applicable laws, regulations, and standards, conducting a gap analysis to identify any areas of non-compliance, implementing necessary changes, and regularly monitoring and auditing network operations to ensure continued compliance. Proper documentation of all activities is essential for demonstrating compliance to auditors and regulatory bodies.

Chapter 8: Exam Preparation

If you've made it this far through the guide, congratulations are in order. You're on the brink of being well-prepared for the CompTIA Network+ exam. But let's not forget, knowledge without proper exam strategy is like a ship without a compass—it may not lead you to your desired destination. This chapter aims to bridge that gap by focusing on targeted exam preparation techniques that will maximize your chances of not just passing but acing the exam.

To begin, let's talk about crafting a study plan. It's not enough to casually skim through your materials and expect to excel on the test day. A well-structured study plan, built around your lifestyle and commitments, can set you on a course for success. Identify the times of day when you're most alert and make those your dedicated study hours. Allocate specific chapters or subjects to different days, keeping some buffer time for unplanned interruptions. Don't just read—actively engage with the material through highlighting, note-taking, and frequent self-assessments.

Speaking of self-assessments, practice exams should be an integral part of your study strategy. The significance of practice exams is twofold. First, they familiarize you with the format and style of the exam. This is crucial for time management and for understanding what to expect on the actual exam day. Second, practice exams serve as a diagnostic tool to identify your areas of weakness. Once you've taken a couple of practice tests, analyze your performance. Pay attention to the questions you got wrong and understand why you got them wrong. This analysis will direct your focus towards areas that need more revision and fortification.

So, you've got your study plan and you're diligently taking practice exams. What else can you do to prepare? Let's talk about simulators and labs. CompTIA Network+ isn't just a test of theoretical knowledge; it's a measure of your practical understanding of networking concepts. Many candidates overlook this and focus solely on bookish knowledge. To truly prepare for all facets of the exam, it's recommended to spend time on network simulators. These platforms emulate real-world networking environments and allow you to practice configuration, troubleshooting, and other hands-on tasks. The experience will boost your confidence and your ability to handle the practical questions on the exam.

The mental aspect of exam preparation is often overlooked but can be equally important. Stress and anxiety can negatively affect your performance. Employ techniques like mindfulness, meditation, or even light physical exercise to keep stress levels in check. Remember, a calm mind absorbs and recalls information more efficiently than a stressed one.

Study Strategies

Let's go in-depth into the points we've raised early;

Creating a Study Plan

The first step in preparing for any exam, including the CompTIA Network+, is to create a study plan. A well-structured study plan will help you organize your time, set achievable goals, and track your progress.

1. Assess Your Current Knowledge: Start by assessing your current knowledge and identifying any gaps. CompTIA provides an exam objectives document that outlines all the topics covered in the exam. Use this document as a checklist to identify areas where you need more study.
2. Set Realistic Goals: Break down the exam objectives into smaller, manageable chunks and set specific goals for each study session. For example, you might decide to focus on IP addressing and subnets one week and then move on to network security the following week.
3. Create a Schedule: Allocate specific times each day or week for studying. Consistency is key, so try to stick to your schedule as much as possible.
4. Select Study Materials: Choose study materials that suit your learning style. There are a variety of resources available, including books, online courses, practice exams, and interactive labs. This guide, of course, is an excellent starting point.
5. Practice, Practice, Practice: Practice exams are a crucial component of your study plan. They help you assess your knowledge, identify areas for improvement, and get comfortable with the exam format.

Mastering the Content

The CompTIA Network+ exam covers a wide range of topics, from basic networking concepts to more advanced topics such as network security and troubleshooting. It is essential to have a thorough understanding of all these areas.

1. Networking Concepts: Begin with the fundamentals, such as the OSI and TCP/IP models, IP addressing, and network topologies. Understanding these concepts is crucial as they form the foundation for more advanced topics.
2. Network Installation and Configuration: Learn about the installation and configuration of networks, including LAN/WAN technologies, wireless networks, and virtualization and cloud computing. Understanding these concepts is crucial for designing and implementing networks in real-world scenarios.
3. Network Operations: Familiarize yourself with network monitoring, configuration management, and network documentation. These are essential skills for maintaining and optimizing network performance.
4. Network Security: Network security is a critical aspect of networking. Understand the basic security concepts, firewalls and IDS/IPS systems, VPNs and remote access, and security policies and compliance.
5. Troubleshooting: Develop your troubleshooting skills by understanding the troubleshooting methodology, identifying network problems, and using the appropriate tools for troubleshooting.

Utilizing Practice Exams

Practice exams are an invaluable resource for preparing for the CompTIA Network+ exam. They allow you to assess your knowledge, identify areas for improvement, and get comfortable with the exam format.

1. Start Early: Begin taking practice exams early in your study process. This will help you assess your baseline knowledge and identify areas where you need to focus your study efforts.
2. Use Multiple Sources: Utilize practice exams from multiple sources to ensure a well-rounded preparation. This guide includes practice exams, but it is also beneficial to use other resources to expose yourself to a broader range of questions.
3. Simulate Exam Conditions: Try to simulate the actual exam conditions as much as possible when taking practice exams. This means timing yourself, completing the exam in one sitting, and minimizing distractions.
4. Review Your Answers: Carefully review your answers after completing each practice exam. Understand why you got a question wrong and revisit the relevant study material to reinforce your knowledge.

5. Track Your Progress: Keep a record of your scores on each practice exam to track your progress over time. This will help you build confidence as you see your scores improve.

Exam Day Tips

After weeks or even months of preparation, the exam day will finally arrive. It is natural to feel nervous, but remember that you have prepared thoroughly and are well-equipped to succeed.

1. Get a Good Night's Sleep: Ensure you get a good night's sleep the night before the exam. A well-rested mind is more alert and better equipped to recall information.
2. Eat a Healthy Meal: Eat a balanced meal before the exam to fuel your body and mind. Avoid too much caffeine, as it can increase anxiety.
3. Arrive Early: Plan to arrive at the exam center at least 30 minutes early. This will give you time to relax, use the restroom, and get settled before the exam begins.
4. Stay Calm and Focused: Take a few deep breaths before starting the exam to calm your nerves. Read each question carefully and eliminate incorrect answers before selecting your response.
5. Manage Your Time: Keep an eye on the clock and pace yourself throughout the exam. If you come across a question that you are unsure about, make a note of it and move on to the next question. You can come back to it at the end if you have time.

Finally, let's touch on some last-minute strategies to seal your preparation. A day before the exam, go through your notes, flashcards, or any summary materials you have. This is not the time for learning new concepts but for reinforcing what you already know. Don't forget to get a good night's sleep; your mind needs to be at its peak performance on exam day. Make sure you have all the necessary identification and paperwork sorted out in advance, so you're not scrambling at the last minute.

In conclusion, the CompTIA Network+ exam is a milestone on your path to a fulfilling career in networking. It's an opportunity to prove your skills and knowledge, and this chapter is designed to ensure you're equipped with the right tools and strategies to do just that. From crafting a detailed study plan to mastering the art of taking practice exams, from honing practical skills through simulators to maintaining your mental well-being—each element is a piece of the puzzle that, when completed, spells success. So go ahead, put these strategies into practice and stride confidently into your examination room. Your future as a certified networking professional is just an exam away.

1. To speed up a laptop, you have a request from a client for the following upgrades: upgrade RAM to 8GB and replacing the existing 500GB hard disk with a 1TB SSD.
   Which of the following should you do FIRST before you can quote a price and timeframe for this job?

A. Price comparison for SATA and NVMe 1TB SSD.

B. Identify the location of the drive bay.

C. Review the contents of the service manual.

D. Determine amount and size of memory modules already installed.

2. A client has requested your expert advice on a gaming laptop with a 15-inch display that will cost about $1,400. Which of the following screen technologies would be the BEST choice for this user?

A. OLED

B. VA

C. TN

D. IPS

3. A client is generally satisfied with the thin and light laptops in use by her sales force, except that they need touch screens for more interactive presentations. Which of the following is the BEST recommendation for this client?

A. Replace the display panels with touch-screen versions.

B. Purchase styluses for use with the existing laptops.

C. Recommend the client never buy laptops from that manufacturer again.

D. Work on a schedule for replacing laptops with touch-screen versions.

4. Your client is asking for your help in deciding between two similar laptop computers. Laptop 1 has a Type-C port according to the marketing literature, while Laptop 2 has a USB 3.1 Gen 2 Type-C port according to its marketing literature. The client needs 10Gbps speed to support an additional display and highspeed USB SSDs connected to a Type-C docking station. Which laptop should you recommend, based on the marketing literature?

A. You don't know how fast either laptop's USB Type-C port is, so either one will do.

B. Laptop 1's Type-C port is faster than Laptop 2's, so you should recommend Laptop 1.

C. Laptop 2's USB Type-C port runs at 10Gbps, but you don't know how fast Laptop 1's USB Type-C port is. Recommending Laptop 2 is the safe choice.

D. Both laptops have the same-speed port but aren't labeled the same. Time to flip a coin?

5. Your client has asked you to buy charging/sync cables for their fleet of current Android and iOS smartphones. These cables will be used with laptops that have only USB-C ports. Identify these connectors and specify which ones to look for when you are shopping.

In the following table, identify the USB-C and Lightning connectors as well as the other connectors shown. The Android charging cables will have USB-C connectors at both ends and the iOS charging cables will have a USB-C connector at one end and Lightning at the other.

The connector types are shown in the first column. Identify each connector type in the second column.

Cable ends	Connector Type
A. 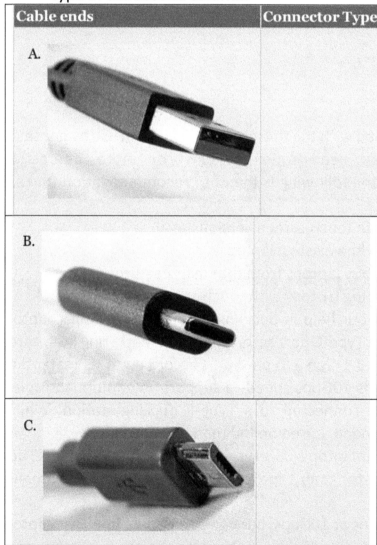	
B.	
C.	

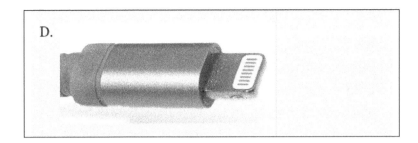

D.

6. Your client is using a Bluetooth speaker with two different computing devices. She calls you because after using the device with her desktop, she was unable to use it with her smartphone, but a new Bluetooth headset does work with her smartphone. Which of the following is the BEST answer as to why the user can't use her speaker with her smartphone?

A. The smartphone's Bluetooth radio has stopped working.

B. The desktop computer needs to shut off its Bluetooth radio to enable the Bluetooth device to connect with another device.

C. The speaker is turned off.

D. The Bluetooth device should be replaced under warranty.

7. Your client is planning to use Google Workspace on a 45-minute flight to prepare his presentation after charging his laptop all day. The presentation will be given within a half-hour of arrival, and very little has been completed yet. Which of the following problems could make the presentation preparation difficult?

A. Running out of power

B. Airplane mode

C. Single-screen display

D. None of the above

8. You are researching the electronic services offered by a bank that your company will begin using next month. You want to make sure that web-based banking users make secure connections to the bank server. Which one of the following protocols would be most appropriate for this use?

A. SSH

B. HTTP

C. HTTPS

D. FTP

9. You are having a discussion with a new hire in your department. The new hire asks you this question: "Which is better, TCP or UDP?" Which of the following is the BEST answer?

A. TCP because it guarantees delivery.

B. UDP because it is faster.

C. TCP or UDP; it makes no difference.

D. TCP or UDP are both important because they do different jobs.

10. Your client has been using POP3 email for several years when she used only a desktop computer. Now, your client has switched to IMAP, but her email client cannot connect to her email box. Her other network and Internet apps work properly. Which of the following is the MOST LIKELY reason for the problem?

A. Her email client must be upgraded to use IMAP.

B. She must buy a subscription to use IMAP.

C. She must delete all of her POP3 email first.

D. She must reconfigure her email client to use the correct ports and servers for IMAP.

11. Your client has been receiving DNS errors frequently. After consulting with you and changing his DNS servers, he is still getting DNS errors on his previous lookups, but new websites are resolving (being translated from URL to IP address and opening) properly. What is the BEST suggestion to fix this problem?

A. Reinstall the DNS server on the network.

B. Flush the DNS cache.

C. Stop using DNS.

D. Switch back to the original DNS servers.

12. A network with multiple servers has two problems: uneven server utilization and excessive numbers of outbound requests from the network for the same Internet content. Which two of the following will help improve network performance?

A. Load balancer

B. SCADA

C. Web server

D. Proxy server

13. Which of the following is most likely to include some IoT devices?

A. Fileshare server

B. SCADA

C. Spam gateway

D. Authentication, authorization, and accounting (AAA)

14. Your client has been reading about the advantages of IPv6 and wants to start using it. However, when she runs ipconfig /all, she sees only an IPv6 address

that starts with fe80, and when she checks her public IP address, it only shows an IPv4 address. What is the reason? Select the best answer from the following:

A. fe80 indicates that IPv6 has failed.

B. A link-local address can't join an IPv6 network.

C. The ISP doesn't support IPv6 yet.

D. She needs to upgrade her network card drivers.

15. A co-worker has just lost Internet connectivity. However, he can still open folders on the network and print to the multifunction printer/scanner/copier/finisher device down the hallway. You ask him to run ipconfig /all to see the current IP address, and it comes up as 169.254.255.6. Which of the following best explains what is going on?

A. The network is broken.

B. The company didn't pay its ISP this month.

C. The DNS server has failed.

D. The DHCP server has failed.

16. Your client has decided to create a second network in her office building for "hoteling" clients who show up occasionally to avoid potential security risks for her own company's network. Which of the following should you recommend to do this?

A. Virtual private network

B. Router

C. Virtual LAN

D. DHCP

17. Your client has been having a lot of problems with email spam and bots. Which of the following DNS records need to be changed to help fight these threats?

A. DHCP lease

B. TXT record

C. A record

D. AAAA record

18. Your client has decided it's time to connect networks in satellite offices around the city. Which of the following are necessary to make this happen?

A. Using a WISP to set up the connection

B. Adding a SAN for storage

C. Using a PAN to connect the computers

D. All of the above

19. A client of yours has moved to a rural area and has asked for your assistance in selecting a broadband provider. The maximum budget per month is $100, the customer needs fast speeds for gaming and video chatting, and the customer expects to download up to 150GB of data per month. The available options include the following:

A. WISP #1 (50Mbps download, unlimited data) $75/month
B. Satellite Internet (30Mbps download, 100GB high-speed data) $100/month
C. Cellular LTE service (25Mbps download, unlimited data) $60/month
D. WISP #2 (75Mbps download, unlimited data) $90/month E. Based on these factors, as well as what you know about the service types, which would you recommend?

20. During the laptop RAM upgrade process (goal: 8GB per system), you determine that some of the computers have 2x2GB SODIMM RAM modules for a total of 4GB onboard, while others have 1x4GB SODIMM RAM modules for a total of 4GB onboard. All systems have two SODIMM sockets. All of the 4GB memory and 2GB memory have the same form factor (DDR3 SODIMM) and timing. There are 10 systems with 1x4GB modules, and 20 systems with 2x2GB modules. Which of the following purchases will provide 8GB of identical RAM per system without considering spares?

A. Buy 30 1x4GB modules.
B. Buy 50 1x4GB modules.
C. Buy 60 1x4GB modules.
D. Buy 10 1x4GB modules.

21. After a break-in and questions about security after working hours, your client has asked you to help add security features to their network. The client has software firewalls running on all computers and several unused Ethernet ports on outside walls. Which of the following recommendations would provide improved security? (Choose all that apply.)

A. Add power next to each Ethernet port to support cameras.
B. Use a PoE switch to provide power to cameras.
C. Add a hardware firewall to the network between the server and the Internet.
D. Add a hardware firewall to the network between the server and its clients.

22. A friend of yours has asked you to help clean out a closet full of miscellaneous network hardware. Your friend is hoping to find a Gigabit Ethernet switch, a DSL modem, and an access point. Which of the following devices can your friend use? (Choose all that apply.)

A. This item is marked 10/100 Ethernet switch.

B. This item is marked 10/100/1000 Ethernet switch.

C. This item has an RJ-11 port, two antennas, and a four-port RJ-45 switch.

D. This item has an RJ-45 port and two antennas.

E. This item has an RJ-45 port and a four-port RJ-45 switch.

23. You are helping a friend set up a wireless network using a surplus 802.11n (Wi-Fi 4) router. Your friend wants to use Channel 149 because there is no wireless network using it. However, only channels 1–11 can be detected by the router. What is the reason?

A. The router is defective and should not be used.

B. The manufacturer must provide a special code to enable three-digit channels.

C. 802.11n routers are not required to support channels above 11.

D. Your friend needs to attach another antenna to the wireless router.

24. Your client wants to use Bluetooth interfacing for a printer, a keyboard, and a headset for listening to music. The computer doesn't have on-board Bluetooth, so purchasing and installing a USB-Bluetooth adapter is necessary. The headset recommends Bluetooth 5 or above, while the printer and keyboard don't specify a particular Bluetooth version. Which of the following is the best strategy to follow?

A. Buy two Bluetooth adapters: Bluetooth 5.1 and an older Bluetooth version.

B. Buy three Bluetooth adapters, one for each device.

C. Buy a Bluetooth 5.1 adapter

D. All of the above strategies will work equally well.

25. Your client is asking for your recommendations for troubleshooting the company network. The company network is using a mixture of wired and wireless clients, and cabling is provided and maintained by the building management. Which of the following network tools should be recommended? (Choose all that apply.)

A. Loopback plug

B. Network tap

C. Wi-Fi analyzer

D. Crimper

26. A different client is planning to replace its obsolete CAT5 cable with CAT6 cable and has purchased a spool of the cable. Which of the following items does this client also need to purchase for this job? (Choose all that apply.)

A. CAT6 connectors

B. Coax crimper

C. TP crimper

D. Coax wire stripper

27. Your client has asked you to add a second 4K display to a PC. The PC currently connects to the first 4K display with DisplayPort (DP). The new 4K display has DP-in, DP-out, and HDMI ports. The PC has a single DisplayPort and two HDMI ports. The cable run between the PC and the existing display is 50 feet, and the new display will be located directly beside the existing display. The second display is already paid for, but you need to select the connection type. The budget for the connection is $50. Which of the following is the BEST recommendation for making this work?

A. Buy a 60-foot 4K HDMI cable to allow sufficient slack.

B. Daisy-chain the second 4K display to the first 4K display with DP or mDP cables.

C. Daisy-chain the second 4K display to the first 4K display with HDMI.

D. Inform the client that you need to purchase a second graphics card and cable.

28. Your company has had a cable failure on an existing 100BaseT (Fast Ethernet) network segment. Plans are to upgrade this segment to Gigabit Ethernet in the next 12 months. Keeping both current and future needs in mind, which of the following is the BEST solution?

A. Replace the current cable with a CAT5 cable now and run CAT5e alongside it for future use.

B. Replace the current cable with a CAT5e cable.

C. Replace the current cable with an RG6QS cable.

D. Replace the current cable with a CAT6 cable.

29. Your client is asking for your help in selecting memory upgrades for their desktop computers. All of the computers use DDR4 memory, but there are four different models in the fleet. The Internet connection at the client site is out for a few days, which is why the upgrade has been scheduled. Of the following strategies, which can best help you determine the upgrades that are necessary?

A. Open one system at random and check its memory size, type, and configuration.

B. Watch all of the computers when they start up and look for memory size information.

C. Open up one system of each model and check its configuration.

D. Run MSInfo32.exe on each system.

30. Your client has asked you to perform a custom desktop build using, as much as possible, leftover parts from previous system upgrades that took place in 2020 or earlier. Some of the parts you can choose from include A motherboard with 240-pin memory slots and an installed AMD CPU A

motherboard with 288-pin memory slots and an installed 7th generation Intel CPU Two matched DDR3 4GB modules Three DDR4 modules, two 8GB, and one 4GB Which of the following builds are most likely to work from the facts listed?

A. 240-pin motherboard with all DDR4 modules
B. 288-pin motherboard with any or all DDR4 modules
C. 288-pin motherboard with pair of DDR3 modules
D. 240-pin motherboard with pair of DDR3 modules

31. You have the following 2TB drives:

1. 7200 RPM SATA
2. SSD SATA 2.5-inch
3. SSD SATA M.2
4. SSD NVMe M.2

You have three desktop systems:

➢ System X has an available SATA host adapter on the motherboard
➢ System Y has an available M.2 interface with an M key
➢ System Z has an available M.2 interface with a B key

Which drive provides the best performance in System X? _____
Which drive provides the best performance in System Y? _____
Which drive provides the best performance in System Z? _____

32. You have 10 systems that need RAID drive installations. Five of these support RAID 0 and 1 only, while the other five support RAID 0, 1, and 10. To provide maximum safety and best performance for all systems and provide RAID array sizes of at least 4TB each, how many identical drives are needed? How large should each drive be? Do not calculate for spares, as they are provided for in a separate budget. Choose the BEST answer from the following possibilities.

➢ 30 drives, 4TB each
➢ 40 drives, 8TB each
➢ 30 drives, 2TB each
➢ 20 drives, 3TB each

33. Your client has located several computer components in a closet and wants you to build a PC using these parts:

➢ AMD CPU
➢ Desktop motherboard with a 2017-vintage LGA CPU socket
➢ PCI video card

Which of the following is the most accurate answer to your client's request?

A. The PCI card will plug into the motherboard.

B. An adapter is needed to enable the CPU to work in the motherboard.

C. These parts can work in a single PC.

D. These parts must be used in separate PCs.

34. Your client needs to add four large-capacity external drives to a media development PC. The drives are USB 3.2 Gen 1 and Gen 2 hard disk drives and SSDs. When the drives were plugged into a USB 3.2 Gen 2 hub, the drives were too slow because they were sharing a single USB controller chip. You recommend a USB 3.2 Gen 2 card with four separate USB controllers (one for each port). However, this card is a PCIe ×4 card, and the computer has a PCIe ×8 and a PCIe ×1 slot available. What should you do?

   A. See if a PCIe ×8 card is available.

   B. See if a PCIe ×1 card is available.

   C. Use the PCIe ×8 slot for the x4 card.

   D. Tell the client to get a new motherboard that includes a PCIe ×4 slot.

35. You are helping a client troubleshoot a Windows 10 system that will not start from the system drive. After doing some research, you determine that the best course of action is to start the system from a diagnostic USB drive that contains a Linux distro. Which of the following BIOS/UEFI settings will make this EASIEST to do?

A. Change boot order

B. Enable TPM

C. Override boot order

D. Enable Secure Boot

36. Your client wants to upgrade her fleet of Windows 10 PCs to run Windows 11. All of them were purchased with TPM installed. However, some are blocking upgrades to Windows 11. Which of the following could cause this issue? (Choose all that apply.)

A. TPM version installed on some systems is TPM 1.2.

B. TPM was not enabled on some systems.

C. Windows 10's TPM is not supported in Windows 11.

D. Secure Boot is not enabled on some systems.

37. Your client has several four-year-old desktop PCs that are being upgraded with more powerful PCIe video cards and higherperformance CPUs. Both draw more power than the current components. The current power supply is a 550-watt power supply that provides 44Amps of 12V power (528 watts).

Which of the following would provide at least 800 watts of 12V power and sell for the lowest price?

➢ Power Supply A: 58Amp 12V, $85
➢ Power Supply B: 70Amp 12V, $99
➢ Power Supply C: 64Amp 12V, $94
➢ Power Supply D: 78Amp 12V, $109

38. You are preparing to install a new high-performance PCIe video card into a computer. Which of the following power leads are you most likely to need to connect to this card?

A

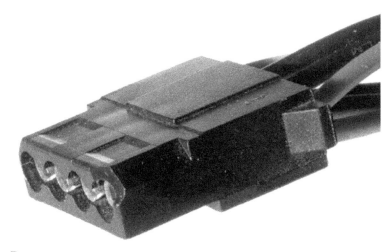

B

C

D

39. Your client has purchased an MFD but didn't use the software provided by the vendor to set up the device. Instead, he let Windows recognize the device and set it up. The copying feature doesn't work. What is the most likely place to start troubleshooting?

A. Test the scanner component.

B. Send back the MFD for replacement.

C. Install the software provided by the vendor.

D. Connect the printer to a USB port instead of the network.

40. You are assisting a user with print quality issues on her inkjet printer. She is attempting to print photos on glossy paper, but the results are streaky and the paper has too much ink on it. Which two settings does she need to check?

A. Duplex
B. Quality
C. Tray
D. Paper type

41. Your client is experiencing a lot of poor-quality printouts from a laser printer. It prints pages on standard copy paper that look OK until they are picked up, and then the print falls off the page. The toner cartridge and imaging drum check out OK. Which other component is likely to be the cause of the problem?

A. The rasterizer that creates the page in the printer
B. Not enough memory in the printer
C. Paper loaded upside down
D. The fuser

42. You have been asked to pick up some consumables for the office. The shopping list contains the following:

A. One spool each of TPA, ABS, and PETG filament in black, white, and blue
B. Cash register tape
C. Black ink cartridge

Choose the types of printers you are shopping for from the following list:

1. Laser
2. Inkjet
3. Impact
4. 3-D
5. Thermal

43. Your client needs to scale up its current IT facilities to handle an expected rush of sales for its new electronic widget. It needs to handle global orders after the latest World of Widgets trade show using its existing software. Which of the following cloud service model types would best meet this need?

A. SaaS
B. Rapid elasticity
C. IaaS
D. PaaS

44. Your company has just signed a contract with a cloud provider to enable field workers to automatically get updates to the current product catalog. Which cloud computing benefit will field workers be enjoying?

A. Rapid elasticity

B. File synchronization

C. Metered utilization

D. High availability

45. Your client is setting up an existing computer to be a virtual machine host for four 64-bit VMs, one running Windows 10, one running Windows 11, and two running Linux, all installed for testing purposes. Which of the following computers would be most suitable?

A. Four-core, eight-thread 3GHz CPU with 16GB RAM, 4TB RAID 1 on Gigabit Ethernet

B. Eight-core, eight-thread 4GHz CPU with 32GB RAM, 2TB SSD on Fast Ethernet

C. Six-core, 12-thread 3.7 GHz CPU with 64GB RAM, 8TB RAID 1 on Wi-Fi 6

D. Two-core, four-thread 2.5GHz CPU with 8GB RAM, 1TB on Wi-Fi 4.

46. Your client is partway through setting up a VMM but is not sure if the CPU has hardware virtualization enabled. Which of the following BIOS/UEFI settings need to be enabled on an Intel CPU?

A. VT-Q

B. SVM

C. Secure Boot

D. VT-x

47. You are working with a user who was experiencing an issue with displaying computer-aided design (CAD) graphics on her computer. You replaced her monitor and performed some tests that showed that the problem is resolved and the user has full system functionality. What should you do next?

A. Document your findings

B. Close the ticket

C. Conduct additional testing

D. Escalate to senior technicians

48. You are helping a user troubleshoot a problem printing to a new all-in-one (AIO) device that was recently installed. The user is unable to print any documents to that printer but is able to print to other devices on the same network. You have researched the problem on the Internet and in your organization's knowledge base (KB), and that research is pointing you to several possible issues. You are working to identify which issue is the most likely culprit. What step are you taking in the troubleshooting process?

A. Verify full system functionality

B. Identify the problem

C. Implement the solution

D. Establish a theory

49. Your client is experiencing frequent system crashes that happen with a mix of applications and tasks. An examination of the computer reveals that there are four possible causes:

A. Memory issues

B. Overdue application and operating system updates

C. Clogged air intakes

D. Power supply overloaded

E. The client is on a deadline (of course!). Which should you address FIRST?

50. You are visiting a client when you notice a desktop computer in a nearby cubicle is making a grinding noise. You mention this problem to your client, and she asks you to take a look. After a quick look at the computer and reviewing the documentation, you realize that the grinding noise is coming from the bottom rear of the computer and that the computer uses an SSD for storage. Which of the following is the most likely source of the noise?

A. Case fan

B. Power supply fan

C. HDD

D. CPU fan

51. Your client is using a RAID 1 array for a data drive and a RAID error message is displayed. What should the client do first?

A. Shut down the computer with the RAID array.

B. Restart the system to see if the error persists.

C. Replace the host adapter.

D. Capture all error messages from the operating system or RAID array.

52. You are installing a new SATA 8TB internal drive as a data drive. The drive will hold critical data and will be backed up with both cloud and local storage. Which of the following would you recommend for early warning of SMART drive failure?

A. Run error-checking regularly.

B. Install the drive vendor's diagnostics utility and run it regularly.

C. Run SMARTST.EXE on each startup.

D. Replace the power supply.

53. Your client occasionally uses an HDTV for classroom presentations. Normally everything works fine, but she has a new laptop and video cable, and when she connected it, there was no picture on the HDTV. Which of the following is the FIRST item to check?

A. New laptop has defective video port.

B. The video cable is defective.

C. Mirroring was not enabled.

D. The new laptop is using a different type of video cable.

54. Your friend has frantically called you with a problem: he can't get his brand-new PCIe graphics card to display anything. He upgraded an older system and had problems connecting the PCIe power lead to the card. When you arrive, you discover that he has inserted a six-pin PCIe power cable into the card that takes eight pins. Which of the following should you look for FIRST?

A. An eight-pin PCIe power cable

B. An adapter to turn a drive power cable into a PCIe power cable

C. A different slot for the PCIe card

D. A replacement power supply

55. Your client has just dunked their water-resistant smartphone in the deep end of the pool. After checking the specifications, your client remembers that the phone has an IP67 rating. Which of the following BEST describes your client's situation?

A. The phone will be fine.

B. The phone is ruined.

C. The phone should be dried out immediately.

D. The phone should be replaced under warranty.

56. Your client is using a Windows computer with a touch screen that is not registering touches consistently. After verifying that the problem is the same whether or not a stylus is used, you recommend checking in which of the following locations in Control Panel or Settings for the calibration settings?

A. East of Access Center

B. Tablet PC Settings

C. Mouse

D. Pen and Touch

57. The laser printer in your office is making a grinding noise. What should you do FIRST?

A. Shut down the printer.

B. Listen to the printer to determine where the noise is coming from.

C. Replace the imaging drum/toner cartridge.

D. Replace the fuser assembly.

58. Your client calls you because the multifunction device is producing speckled pages. Which question should you ask FIRST to help troubleshoot the problem?

A. Are all printouts affected or only printouts made when copying a document?

B. Is this a laser or inkjet device?

C. How old is the toner cartridge or imaging drum?

D. Does the printer use an ink cartridges or ink tanks?

59. Your client has a Gigabit Ethernet network that is connected using CAT5e cabling. Some of the network cabling is running close to a flickering fluorescent light fixture, and users are complaining about slow network performance. Which of the following should you try FIRST to improve performance?

A. Replace UTP cable with STP cable.

B. Replace STP cable with UTP cable.

C. Enable QoS in the router.

D. Repair the fluorescent light fixture.

60. Your client's small-office network has limited connectivity. Which of the following router functions has stopped working?

A. QoS

B. LSO

C. DHCP

D. IPv4

61. When you're installing a new hardware device on a Windows 10 Pro system, what must be present before the OS will support the device?

A. USB hub

B. Signed device driver

C. BIOS/UEFI support for the device

D. PnP support

62. Which one of the 64-bit Windows 10 editions does not support up to 512 GB of primary memory?

A. Enterprise

B. Pro

C. Home

D. Pro for Workstations

63. In a Windows environment, what is a domain?

A. A logical grouping of network servers, nodes, and resources.

B. A peer-to-peer network

C. A grouping of workstations from remote networks

D. A workgroup

64. Which Windows 10 edition is limited to settings and configurations for a local computer only using the Group Policy Editor?

A. Pro

B. Enterprise

C. Pro for Workstations

D. Home

65. What is the type of upgrade process most commonly used to apply new features to a supported Windows edition?

A. Feature update

B. Cumulative update

C. In-place upgrade

D. Servicing stack update

66. What Windows command prompt command verifies system files, folders, and paths and replaces corrupt versions?

A. chkdsk

B. gpupdate

C. sfc

D. ipconfig

67. You are unable to remove all the contents of an existing hard disk using Disk Management. Which command should you use instead?

A. format

B. diskpart

C. gpupdate

D. gpresult

68. A user calls you to ask for help with her network connection. To find out what her network settings are, which of the following commands should you run?

A. ping

B. netstat

C. net use

D. ipconfig

69. You need to use ping to check the connectivity to network server 164.172.1.150, also known as MyServer.net. Which of the following is the correct syntax?

A. ping //MyServer.net

B. ping 164-172-1-150

C. ping MyServer.net

D. ping theserverforthisnetwork

70. You are providing telephone support to a user named Miranda who needs to access her personal folders at a command prompt. From her Users folder, which of the following commands would she need to use to get to her personal folders?

A. cd \Miranda

B. Miranda.exe

C. ls Miranda

D. cd Miranda

71. 1. Some Task Manager tasks or services can be executed from a command prompt. Which of the following commands can be used to execute or kill a task? (Choose two.)

A. net start <service>

B. net stop <service>

C. net kill <service>

D. net execute <service>

E. taskstart <service>

72. Which of the following is not one of the four sections of the Event Viewer?

A. Summary of Administrative Events

B. Recently Viewed Nodes

C. Log Summary

D. Future Events

73. Two primary sections are available when the Local Group Policy Editor first opens: the Computer Configuration and which of the following?

A. User Configuration

B. Local Configuration

C. Group Configuration

D. Network Configuration

74. What system utility should be used to investigate a failed device that is causing problems for a Windows system?

A. Device Manager

B. Configuration Manager

C. System Information

D. Disk Management

75. Which of the following is not one of the five main keys of the Windows Registry?

A. HKEY_CLASSES_ROOT

B. HKEY_CURRENT_USERS

C. HKEY_LOCAL_MACHINE

D. HKEY_USERS

E. HKEY_CURRENT_CONFIG

76. What Control Panel option is used to configure the Internet security zone for a given scenario?

A. System

B. File Explorer Options

C. Security Options

D. Internet Options

77. Which Control Panel option do you select to access the media streaming settings?

A. Internet Options

B. AutoPlay

C. Network and Sharing Center

D. Sync Center

78. What Control Panel option provides for centralized viewing and management of monitors, printers, and peripheral devices?

A. Devices and Printers

B. Printers and Devices

C. Device Manager

D. Programs and Features

79. What Windows 10 applet allows a user to modify a computer's tools, features, and settings?

A. Utility Manager

B. Control Panel

C. System Information

D. MMC

80. Windows 10 Power Settings are configured from which category of the Control Panel?

A. Appearance and Personalization

B. Clock, Language, and Region

C. User Accounts

D. System and Security

81. A customer is having trouble reading the text on their computer screen because it is too small. What setting in the Settings Display app can you use to adjust the size of the text, apps, and other items?

A. Scale and layout

B. Display resolution

C. Display orientation

D. HDR color 2.

82. Which of the following is not a setting that can be configured on the System settings Display option?

A. Brightness

B. Background tint

C. Scaling

D. Resolution

E. HDR color

83. 3. You are setting up a new mobile PC for an in-house client and need to configure the settings that personalize the PC's display, sound, and battery. What section of the Settings app should you use for these settings?

A. Display

B. Personalization

C. System

D. Devices

84. The Diagnostics & Feedback settings are found in which section of the Settings app?

A. Privacy

B. Accounts

C. Devices

D. Optimization

85. On what Windows 10/11 app are the settings for the image or color of the Lock Screen found?

A. System

B. Apps

C. Control Panel

D. Settings

86. A user needs to access a network printer but only knows the network printer's IP address. What should you tell the user?

A. Find the printer brand and model.

B. Use a wireless connection to the printer.

C. The IP address is the only information needed to use the printer.

D. Find out the host name.

87. A Windows user has just returned from a trip during which she connected to the Internet via Wi-Fi networks in coffee shops and airport lounges. The user wants to connect to the new wireless LAN to print a report to a network printer she has used before, but she can't connect to the printer. Which of the following is the most likely cause?

A. Windows Firewall is set for a private network.

B. Windows Firewall is set for a public network.

C. The user must reinstall the printer driver.

D. A printer app can't work on a wireless LAN.

88. You are performing telephone support with a user who has lost his Internet connection on a SOHO network. After running ipconfig, the user reports his IP address as 169.254.0.23. Which of the following should you check first?

A. Broadband modem

B. Network switch

C. Network hub

D. Network router

89. A client says she needs to access an important document that was sent to her over the Internet by one of her clients, but no matter how many times the document has been sent, it never arrives on her computer. What should you check first when resolving this problem?

A. Network adapter

B. Network router

C. Network firewall rules

D. Proxy server

90. A company salesperson is telecommuting from home three days a week. She is setting up a home office but cannot connect to any IP address beyond her home network's router. She ran an ipconfig command and learned that the IP address assigned to her computer is 169.254.0.1. What do you believe to be the source of her problem?

A. No connection to the DHCP server or DHCP server is faulty.

B. The network adapter is faulty.

C. The default gateway is configured incorrectly.

D. The proxy server settings are incorrect.

91. A user is trying to install a 64-bit Windows app on a system running a 32- bit version of Windows. Which of the following recommendations should you make?

A. Use the Program Compatibility Wizard.

B. Create a Program Files (x64) folder for the program.

C. Use the Compatibility tab.

D. Install a 32-bit version of the app.

92. You are preparing a laptop for a trip that involves 12 hours of flight time. You have purchased a software key card from a retail store to use on the trip. When should you install the app?

A. On the flight

B. Before leaving for the airport

C. While waiting for the flight

D. Any of the above are acceptable

93. Your department is preparing to evaluate a new app that has a minimum requirement of 4 GB of RAM but recommends 8 GB of RAM. The systems you want to use have 4 GB of RAM and are expandable to 16 GB. Which of the following will help you evaluate the software most fairly?

A. Set up a large pagefile on each system.

B. Install the software on all computers and see how slow it runs.

C. Install upgrades to 8 GB on some systems and install the app on all systems for comparison.

D. Look for software that runs with 4 GB of RAM.

94. Although your department is now running Windows 10, it relies on an application made for Windows 7. It doesn't run properly on Windows 10. Which of the following could be used to help it run correctly?

A. Device Manager

B. System Properties

C. Compatibility tab

D. Virtual memory

95. Your employer wishes to install a multifactor authentication (MFA) system to control physical access into the company's IT center. Which of the following methods would be perhaps the most convenient way for employees to learn and work with the new system and also be the most secure?

A. One-time passwords (OTPs)

B. External hardware token (key fob)

C. Password

D. Issue keys for new locks on the IT doors.

96. What type of OS is more robustly configured than a home OS and better serves the operating needs of nodes on a centrally managed network?

A. Home workstations

B. Business workstations

C. Network routers

D. Smartphones and tablets

97. You have been delegated the task of picking an operating system for the endpoint workstations of your company's LAN. You wish to ensure that the applications that run on this OS are compatible with the applications running on the networks of the company's product partners. What OS would you recommend?

A. Windows

B. Linux

C. macOS

D. Chrome OS

98. What is the operating system that the macOS is based on?

A. Windows

B. Android

C. UNIX

D. Chrome OS

99. Which of the following are the most popular OSs for smartphones and tablet PCs? (Choose two.)

A. Windows Mobile

B. Google Android

C. Apple iOS

D. Linux Mobile

100. Which of the following are the most common file systems for the Linux OS? (Choose two.)

A. exFAT

B. ext3

C. NTFS

D. ext4

E. APFS

101. You are upgrading a PC from Windows 10 to Windows 11 and have executed the Microsoft PC Health Check, which indicates that the hardware requirements for Windows 11 are met. What should now be the next step in the process?

A. Proceed with the upgrade.

B. Remove all unsigned drivers.

C. Back up all user data and settings.

D. Run the PC Health Check again to verify its results.

102. Which of the following is required for a network boot?

A. USB boot media

B. PXE-compatible network adapter

C. Remote network installation server

D. BIOS/UEFI boot priority for a flash memory device

103. What is the form of copy of an existing installation saved as one file?

A. Image

B. Full copy

C. Incremental backup

D. Differential backup

104. What type of partitioned disks have the tangible limits of capacity not larger than 2.2 TB and no more than four partitions?

A. MBR

B. GPT

C. GUID

D. FAT32

105. What type of disk partition is assigned a drive letter such as C:, E:, or X:?

A. Extended

B. Physical

C. Logical

D. Virtual

106. A macOS user needs to search for a specific file. Which utility should he use?

A. Spotlight

B. Finder

C. Remote Disk

D. Dock

107. A macOS user needs to stop an unresponsive app. What macOS feature can be used to stop the application?

A. Finder

B. Force Quit

C. Terminal

D. Mission Control

108. What is the macOS app used to create backups and snapshots?

A. Time Machine

B. Spotlight

C. Dock

D. Disk Utility

109. Which of the following is a macOS scripting tool used to create scripts used for running an app in background?

A. Time Machine

B. Dock

C. Spotlight

D. launchd

110. What macOS app stores passwords and account details?

A. Dock

B. Finder

C. Keychain Access

D. iCloud

111. A Linux user is trying to update her system's apps with the command apt-get update, but the command doesn't work. What did the user forget to do?

A. Restart in Safe Mode.

B. Run the command from Terminal.

C. Run the command as the root user with sudo.

D. Create an image backup first.

112. A Linux user needs to stop a process but doesn't know its PID. Which command from a Terminal command line would provide this information?

A. ifconfig

B. ps

C. ls

D. kill

113. A backup script created on a Linux system is to run at a particular time of the day. Which Linux command can be used to ensure this occurs as scheduled?

A. backup

B. cron

C. dd

D. grep

114. What Linux command can be executed from a Terminal command line to display the amount of free disk space available on a file system?

A. free

B. chkdsk

c. df

D. ls

115. What system protocol can be used to allow a Linux system to interact with a Windows system to share files and other resources?

A. apt-get

B. dig

C. Samba

D. top

116. Which of the following is a useful feature in the use of access control vestibules (or mantraps) and entry control rosters?

A. Key fob

B. Security guard

C. Biometric lock

D. Cable lock

117. An organization has contacted you for help in stopping security breaches on its servers. The latest breach involved the use of a flash drive to steal credentials. Which of the following is designed to stop this type of security breach?

A. Privacy screen

B. Server lock

C. Cable lock

D. USB lock

118. RFID, magnetic strip, barcode, and QR code technologies can all be used by which of the following?

A. Badge reader

B. Smart card

C. ACLs

D. Biometric lock

119. A Kensington lock connector is used by which of the following devices?

A. Door lock

B. USB lock

C. Cable lock

D. Biometric lock

120. A company wishes to allow its employees to connect their personal devices to its internal network. What software-provided management system should the company consider implementing?

A. Soft tokens

B. Biometric security

C. Mobile device management

D. Smart cards

121. If you log in to a server with your username and password, which type of authentication is being used?

A. Multifactor

B. TACACS+

C. Single factor

D. WEP

122. WPA3-Enterprise uses which of the following for authentication?

A. SAE

B. TKIP

C. AES

D. WPA2

123. What is the authentication technology used to authenticate a user web content request without needing to send a password over the Internet?

A. SAE

B. TACACS+

C. Kerberos

D. MFA

124. Entering a code sent to a device along with a user name and password constitutes which type of authentication?

A. RADIUS authentication

B. Multifactor authentication

C. Single-factor authentication

D. WEP

125. Which of the following statements is true of AES encryption? (Choose two.)

A. It features 128-bit, 192-bit, and 256-bit encryption.

B. It is easily defeated.

C. It is the strongest wireless encryption standard.

D. It is the weakest wireless encryption standard.

126. A client calls you for help: the company files are encrypted and they'll be deleted unless the company sends a payment in cryptocurrency. What type of attack has happened to your client?

A. Malware

B. Trojan

C. Worm

D. Ransomware

127. Instructing individuals in your company not to click URLs in suspicious e-mails is an example of what?

A. Social engineering

B. Paranoia

C. End-user education

D. Untrusted software

128. If anti-malware software is a second line of system defense, what would be an organization's first line of defense against malware and social engineering attacks?

A. Antivirus software

B. Third-party consultants

C. Risk assessment policies

D. End-user training and education

129. A company's electrical power costs have suddenly increased significantly without any major equipment changes to the system. What could one possibility be for this increase?

A. Hardware failures

B. Rogue cryptominers

C. Software failures

D. Faulty distribution equipment

130. Which of the following OSs provide some form of a recovery mode?

A. Windows

B. Android

C. macOS

D. All of the above

131. A client reports that the organization's wireless network is being flooded with pings and page requests far beyond normal limits. The pings and page requests are coming from a wide variety of locations. Your client is dealing with what type of attack?

A. DDoS

B. Impersonation

C. DoS

D. Social engineering

132. You receive an e-mail purporting to be from the head of IT that is asking you to install a piece of malware. Which type of attack is being used?

A. Impersonation

B. Spoofing

C. Evil twin

D. Brute force

133. Security cameras reveal that someone is walking by the server room and pulling reports out of the trash. What is going on?

A. Dumpster diving

B. Shoulder surfing

C. Phishing

D. Vishing

134. The same day that your accounting software vendor is informed of a security vulnerability, you discover it was used to attack accounts payable. What type of attack is being attempted?

A. Phishing

B. On-path

C. Zero day

D. Cross-site scripting (XSS)

135. The RADIUS authentication server on your wireless network has been hacked and a list of old passwords has been leaked. Although none of the passwords are current, the list could still be used for which of the following attacks?

A. Brute force

B. Whaling

C. SQL injection

D. Dictionary

136.   You have been using a separate and unique login username and password for several different Microsoft applications, including Xbox Live. You learn that you can use just one login account for all Microsoft products. What is it?

A. Administrator account

B. Remote user account

C. Microsoft account

D. Guest account

137.   A client has called you needing help to find BitLocker on a Windows 10 Home edition PC. The client wants to encrypt a hard disk drive and was unable to find it. What is your response to this client?

A. Set File Explorer to show hidden files.

B. Search the Web for how to edit the Registry.

C. Look in the PC's documentation.

D. BitLocker is not installed with Windows 10/11 Home editions.

138.   Which one of the following is not currently a Windows 10/11 sign-in option?

A. Windows Hello

B. Security Key

C. Password

D. Picture Password

E. Spoken Password

139.   What is the user sign-on type that authenticates a user only once on a device or network and allows access to multiple applications or services?

A. Windows Hello

B. SSO

C. Security key

D. Password

140.   An administrator is suspicious that unknown and unsigned applications are being installed by a user on a network node. What UAC setting should the administrator use to block users from installing software on their computers?

A. Always notify me when

B. Notify me only when apps try to make changes to my computer (default)

C. Notify me only when I make changes to my computer

D. Never notify

141. You are considering using one of the following eight-character passwords. Which is the strongest password?

A. 12345678

B. 1Z$#7j!~

C. 867530900

D. My$$Name

142. Your client is being plagued by a series of brute-force logon attacks. Which of the following group policy settings would best help stop them?

A. Account Lockout Policy

B. Security Options

C. Password Policy

D. Logon Time Restrictions

143. Your department was recently attacked by malware that was automatically loaded from a consultant's USB drive when it was inserted for diagnostic purposes. Which of the following should be disabled?

A. Plug and Play

B. File Explorer

C. AutoPlay

D. BIOS/UEFI

144. You wish to prevent users from using the same password over and over. What setting do you need to configure to prevent the same password from being reused within a one-year period?

A. Enforce Password History

B. Maximum Password Age

C. Minimum Password Length

D. Relax Minimum Length Requirement

145. Data that is stored on a computer or mobile device, a database server, or an external backup medium is considered to be which of the following?

A. Data in transit

B. Data in use

C. Data in suspense

D. Data at rest

146. An Android phone with confidential company information was lost. The information on the phone began to be used for attacks on company resources, although the user had set up a passcode. Which of the following Android settings could have prevented attacks using the information in the phone? (Choose two.)

A. Remote wipe

B. Firewall

C. Device encryption

D. BYOD

147. A client is attempting to sign on to his iPhone but cannot remember the passcode. He has tried eight times and the wait time keeps getting longer between attempts. What would you advise him to do?

A. Keep trying to log in.

B. Stop trying until he can get back home and check to see if he has the information available there.

C. Use a hacking tool.

D. Run antivirus.

148. You are part of a team developing a BYOD policy for smartphone usage. Which of the following topics is most likely to be part of the policy?

A. Approved case colors

B. Ownership of private data stored on the device

C. Ownership of charging cables

D. Ownership of company data stored on the device

149. What biometric method compares a camera-captured image of a user's face to an image previously captured from a scanned photograph and stored?

A. Facial recognition

B. Faceprinting

C. Image matching

D. Pattern matching

150. The Internet of Things (IoT) is a communications network of devices. What is the primary component in each device for its operations and communications?

A. Embedded device

B. Modem

C. Microcontroller

D. Integrated circuit

151. A 64-GB flash memory card contains confidential information. Which of the following methods ensures that data cannot be read from the card and that the card cannot be reused?

A. Drilling

B. Zero-fill

C. Drive wiping

D. Degaussing

152. After the completion of a government contact, your firm must prove that the media used to store data have been destroyed. Which of the following do you need?

A. Drill

B. Certificate of destruction

C. Shredder

D. Degausser

153. Your client is panicking because a disgruntled employee performed some type of command on an important hard drive before leaving the premises. Which of the following would make the data the most difficult to recover?

A. Standard format

B. Zero-fill

C. Drive wiping

D. Low-level format

154. You are in charge of a project to remove hard drives from end-of-life systems and prepare them for donation to schools for reuse. You discover that one of your assistants is running the Format command on each drive before removing it. Which of the following is the best reaction to this discovery?

A. "Good job! No one can get to that data now."

B. "Did you use quick or standard format?"

C. "Using Format isn't drive wiping."

D. "You should be using a drill."

155. Your firm has a large amount of magnetic tape from old mainframe systems. Which of the following is the quickest way to render this tape unreadable?

A. Drilling

B. Zero-fill

C. Drive wiping

D. Degaussing

156. What settings on a new wireless router or AP should be changed immediately after installation? (Choose all that apply.)

A. Brand and model

B. Default administrator login name

C. Default administrator password

D. Location

157. Which of the following programs are you most likely to use when you set up your SOHO router?

A. Web browser

B. Paint program

C. FTP program

D. Word processor

158. What enables you to open a port in the firewall and direct incoming traffic on that port to a specific IP address?

A. Port forwarding

B. Screened subnet

C. Disabling ports

D. Changing channels

159. Which one of the following is not a role fulfilled by a screened subnet on an internal network?

A. Access router

B. Internal router

C. Perimeter router

D. WAN router

160. A local insurance agency wants to block both incoming and outgoing network traffic addressed to one or more specific IP addresses. What feature should the agency configure on its router or firewall?

A. DHCP

B. IP filtering

C. Encryption settings

D. Content filtering

161. A client downloaded a relatively unknown browser called WebWeave, which claims to provide higher security than other, better-known browsers, from a software download site called Apps2Bad.us. He says that since he installed the browser, he is unable to open files in his Windows User folder. What is likely contributing to this situation? (Choose two.)

A. A possibly untrusted site

B. Malware

C. Improper installation

D. User permissions

162. What is the term for software enhancements that add new features or functions to a browser?

A. Add-ons

B. Apps

C. Extensions

D. Plug-ons

163. What browser-related program is an additional feature that becomes a part of a browser for functions like viewing specific types of information?

A. Extension

B. Plug-in

C. Attachment

D. Upgrade

164. Before you fill in the data requested by a form on a web page, what indicator should you look for on the browser's address bar?

A. An anchor symbol

B. A heart symbol

C. A padlock symbol

D. A crossed out insect symbol

165. Sheila wants to be able to access her e-mail account using the same client as she uses on her desktop computer. She receives consulting engagement assignments via e-mail and wants to be able to respond as quickly as possible, even when she is away from her office. What process should she use?

A. E-mail forwarding

B. Synchronization

C. Separate e-mail addresses for her desktop and mobile devices

D. Mirroring

166. To change the boot order, which of the following is necessary?

A. Starting Windows in Safe Mode

B. Restarting the system and opening the BIOS/UEFI firmware setup

C. Using the Task Manager

D. Using MSConfig

167. Which of the following is the best way to recover from a bad device driver update?

A. Rolling back the system

B. Restarting the system and opening the BIOS/UEFI firmware setup

C. Rolling back the device driver

D. Restarting in Safe Mode

168. Your client needs to restart a system to solve a problem. Which of the following should be done first?

A. Creating a registry backup

B. Running System Restore

C. Creating a full system backup

D. Unplugging USB drives

169. Your personal computer used to load your Desktop in about ten seconds. Now it takes ten minutes. Which of the following is not a likely cause?

A. Too many tasks running

B. Malware

C. System file corruption

D. User profile corrupted

170. Which of the following is not an option for the WinRE Troubleshooting Advanced Options?

A. System Restore

B. System Image Recovery

C. System Startup Repair

D. Safe Mode Repair

171. 1. A user navigates to her bank's website, which opens with a padlock icon on the address bar. However, as the user navigates through the bank's website, she notices that the padlock icon has changed to an alert symbol. What is likely the cause for this change?

A. Malware has caused the user to open a page without a trusted certificate.

B. The user is no longer on the home page of the bank.

C. The browser has an issue loading the page.

D. There is a problem with the network router.

172. A user's network host computer is unable to contact any address on the Internet. The user sees that an IPv4 address of 169.254.0.1 is assigned to the computer. What could be the problem?

A. The network adapter must be faulty.

B. The gateway router is down.

C. An APIPA address cannot be used beyond a local network.

D. The URL is bad.

173. What is the term for a displayed warning or error message that results from an antivirus program erroneously flagging legitimate and secure software as malware?

A. False flag

B. False alert

C. False negative

D. True negative

174. Which of the following message types would be used to display an alert that warns against the consequences of an action and asks the user to confirm they wish to continue?

A. Confirmation message

B. Information message

C. Warning message

D. Error message

E. Service message

175. A website keeps displaying small pages requesting information that isn't consistent with the site's content. What type of artifact is being displayed?

A. Web page form

B. Pop-up

C. Hypertext link

D. Web survey

176. After updating anti-malware software and using scanning/removal techniques, what is another step that might be necessary in remediation?

A. Educating the user

B. Repairing damage from malware

C. Re-enabling system restore

D. Creating a restore point

177. Which of the following is a reason to use a clean boot environment in removing malware?

A. It makes the computer run faster.

B. It makes user education easier.

C. It prevents reinfection.

D. It helps prevent malware from interfering with removal.

178. When should you enable System Restore and create a restore point?

A. Before removing malware

B. Before scheduling scans and running updates

C. After scheduling scans and running updates

D. As the last step in the process

179. Determining that a system has probably been infected with malware is which step in the malware removal process?

A. Step 7

B. Step 2

C. Step 3

D. Step 1

180. After you have completed the seven-step malware remediation process, Windows will not start properly. What should be your next steps? (Choose two.)

A. Boot into WinPE.

B. Use WinRE.

C. Boot into the anti-malware app.

D. Repeat the seven-step process.

181. Which of the following issues can be helped by performing a soft reset of a mobile device?

A. Extremely short battery life

B. Slow performance

C. Moisture

D. Display too bright

182. Which of the following services, functions, or features can be used to stop an app or service running in background?

A. Kill app

B. Quit app

C. Force stop

D. Cancel app

183. A mobile device app is failing to update. Which of the following conditions could be the cause? (Choose all that apply.)

A. Insufficient storage space

B. Required service is missing

C. Incompatible with device's OS

D. Conflicts with competitor's app already installed

184. A client has brought a smartphone to you requesting help in determining the battery that should be installed in the device. You consider how the user will use the device and the amount of operating time required to come to the amount of power required. How much additional power should be added to your findings to cover the reduction in the power capacity over the battery's lifetime?

A. 10 percent

B. 20 percent

C. 30 percent

D. 50 percent

185. Your tablet PC cannot establish a connection with a Wi-Fi network. You have checked that the network is configured on the device and is within range for a connection. You are puzzled because you were able to make this connection before a recent airline trip. What should be your next action?

A. Check the network adapter configuration

B. Ping the gateway router

C. Disable Airplane mode

D. Reboot the system

186. High resource utilization when no apps are open could be a sign of which of the following?

A. Dying battery

B. Malware

C. Airplane mode

D. GPS enabled

187. A client has discovered what appears to be a very advanced app that performs data analysis on a mobile device, but the APK must be downloaded from an untrusted site using a URL from a foreign country. If the client downloads this file, what action is being used?

A. Phishing

B. Sideloading

C. Jailbreaking

D. Rooting

188. What advanced configuration setting should only be used in the creation of apps and should not be routinely enabled?

A. Root access

B. Sideloading

C. AirDrop

D. Developer mode

189. Jane is experiencing extremely slow performance on her smartphone. She explains that this has just started about a week ago and just after she let her younger brother use her phone while she was busy. She suspects that he downloaded a game from an untrusted site. What tool can she use to verify her suspicions that the game was a Trojan and her phone is infected with malware? (Choose two.)

A. Data usage monitor

B. Anti-malware app

C. Developer mode

D. Troubleshooting app

190. The act of rooting (accessing the root of) a smartphone may have which of the following results?

A. Releasing the actions of a rootkit

B. Voiding the device's warranty

C. Erasing certain apps

D. Nothing

191. At a minimum, a network topology diagram should record which of the following?

A. Connections between network components such as routers, switches, and WAPs

B. User names and accounts

C. Routing details

D. DHCP address ranges

192. You have been tasked with creating a knowledge base for the Windows-based equipment in your department. Some of the computers were hand-built by a computer shop, and you need to find out the motherboard, chipset, CPU, and RAM information. Which of the following will enable you to find the most information about each system?

A. Contacting the computer shop

B. Dismantling each custom-built PC

C. Running a third-party system information app

D. Viewing the System Properties dialog box

193. Which of the following is not likely to be covered in an acceptable use policy (AUP)?

A. Password handling

B. Keyboard lighting

C. Using e-mail

D. Personal print jobs

194. You are creating an asset tag design for your employer, which plans to use a handheld scanner as part of the company's inventory system. Which of the following must be on the asset tag?

A. Company slogan

B. Manufacturer's serial number

C. Company logo

D. Asset number

   195. Which of the following should be in an organization's knowledge base? (Choose two.)

A. Office floorplan

B. Equipment inventory with descriptions and identification details

C. Network topology diagram

D. End-user login credentials

   196. A rollback plan is used to perform which of the following tasks?

A. Gaining change board approval

B. Analyzing the effects of change

C. Returning to pre-change conditions

D. Aiding end-user acceptance.

   197. Which of the following would be an action in a good change management policy?

A. End users are introduced to a new technology without training.

B. The change board is not consulted during the process.

C. Rumors abound about the reasons for the change.

D. Risk analysis is performed.

   198. Six months after a software change was made in a department, you are asked to troubleshoot a problem. The only related information you can locate refers to the old software system. Which of the steps in change management was not performed?

A. Document changes

B. End-user acceptance

C. Risk management

D. Plan for change

   199. Your organization is proposing a change that will have a big impact on its salespeople in the field. Which of the following steps is most likely to enable the field reps to provide input about the proposed change?

A. Plan for change

B. Risk management

C. End-user acceptance

D. Document changes

200. What individual should be appointed to manage and oversee the implementation plan's activities?

A. Programmer

B. IT manager

C. Change board member

D. Responsible staff member

Answers to Exam Questions

1. C. Review the contents of the service manual.
2. C. TN
3. D. Work on a schedule for replacing laptops with touch-screen versions.
4. C. Laptop 2's USB Type-C port runs at 10Gbps, but you don't know how fast Laptop 1's USB Type-C port is. Recommending Laptop 2 is the safe choice.
5. The correct connector pairing for the Android smartphones is B–B (Type-C connector at both ends). The correct connector pairing for the Apple iPhone is B–D (Type-C to Lightning).
6. B. The desktop computer needs to shut off its Bluetooth radio to enable the Bluetooth device to connect with another device.
7. B. Airplane mode
8. C. HTTPS
9. D. TCP and UDP are both important because they do different jobs.
10. D (reconfigure email client to use IMAP)
11. B (flush the DNS cache)
12. A and D. Load balancer, Proxy server
13. B. SCADA
14. C. The ISP doesn't support IPv6 yet
15. D. The DHCP server has failed
16. C. Virtual LAN
17. B. TXT record
18. A. Using a WISP to set up the connection
19. D. WISP #2, 75Mbps download, unlimited data, $90/month
20. B. Buy 50 1x4GB modules
21. B (use a PoE switch to provide power to cameras), and C (add a hardware firewall to the network between the server and the Internet)
22. B (10/100/1000 Gigabit Ethernet switch), C (DSL modem), and D (access point)
23. C. 802.11n routers are not required to support channels above 11
24. C. Buy a Bluetooth 5.1 adapter
25. B (network tap) and C (Wi-Fi analyzer)
26. A (CAT 6 connectors) and C (TP crimper)
27. B (daisy-chaining displays using DP/mDP)
28. D (replace current cable with CAT6)
29. C. Open up one system of each model and check its configuration.
30. B. 288-pin motherboard with any or all DDR4 modules.

31. System X: Option 2 (SSD SATA 2.5-inch) System Y: Option 4 (SSD NVMe M.2 System Z: Option 3 (SSD SATA M.2)

32. This question is designed to test your understanding of RAID levels and how RAID array sizes are calculated.

Option A, 30 drives at 4TB each, works out like this. RAID 0 provides no data security for any systems, so it can be dismissed for all calculations. RAID 1, which uses two identical drives and provides a mirror of one drive to another for data safety, is supported by five systems, so 10 drives are required. RAID 10, supported by five systems, is safer and faster than RAID 1 and requires four identical drives per system. Thus, 20 drives are needed. The total identical drives needed are 30 (10+20). To achieve a RAID array of 4TB in RAID 1, each drive must be 4TB. Four 4TB drives in a RAID 10 array actually create an 8TB array, but that's acceptable.

Option B, 40 drives at 8TB each, works out this way. There would be 10 unused drives, the RAID 1 array size is 8TB, and the RAID 10 array is 16TB. It exceeds the number of drives and the array size needed, so it's more expensive than needed.

Option C, 30 drives at 2TB each, calculates out this way. The number of drives provides enough for each array. However, the RAID 1 arrays are only 2TB, and the RAID 10 arrays are 4TB. The RAID 10 arrays meet the specifications, but not the RAID 1 arrays.

Option D, 20 drives at 3TB each, doesn't include enough drives to take care of both the RAID 1 and RAID 10 systems. If the drives were used only for RAID 10 arrays, each array would be 6TB, but if 10 more drives were purchased to provide enough drives for the RAID 1 systems, the RAID 1 arrays would be only 3TB each.

Correct Answer: A. 30 drives, 4TB each

33. D. These parts must be used in separate PCs

34. C. Use the PCIe ×8 slot for the x4 card.

35. C. Override boot order J

36. A (TPM version installed on some systems is TPM 1.2), B (TPM was not enabled on some systems), D (Secure Boot is not enabled on some systems)

37. B. 70Amp 12V, $99

38. D. Figure D: PCIe power cable

39. C, Install the software provided by the vendor

40. B, Quality, and D, Paper type

41. D. The fuser is the cause of the problem. Its job is to melt the toner to the paper. If it fails, the toner stays on the paper but will fall off when the paper is picked up, or even blow off the paper if there's any air movement by the printer.

42. 2, 4, 5. Inkjet printer, 3-D printer, Thermal printer

43. C. IaaS

44. B. File synchronization

45. C. Six-core, 12-thread 3.7GHz CPU with 64GB RAM, 8TB RAID 1 on Wi-Fi 6

46. D. VT-x

47. A. Document your findings

48. D. Establish a theory

49. C. Clogged air intakes

50. B. Power supply fan

51. D. Capture all error messages from the operating system or RAID array

52. B. Install the drive vendor's diagnostics utility and run it regularly.

53. D. The new laptop is using a different type of video cable.

54. A. An eight-pin PCIe power cable

55. C. The phone should be dried out immediately.

56. B. Tablet PC Settings

57. B. Listen to the printer.

58. A. Are all printouts affected or only printouts made when copying?

59. D, Repair the fluorescent light fixture

60. C, DHCP

61. B, Windows requires a Microsoft signed device driver for all installed devices.

62. C, Windows Home 64-bit edition supports only 128 GB of RAM.

63. A, A domain is a logical grouping of network servers, nodes, and resources.

64. D, The Home edition cannot create settings for multiple computers through the Active Directory.

65. C, The in-place upgrade process is used to apply new features to a supported Windows edition.

66. C, The sfc command verifies system files, folders, and paths and replaces corrupt versions.

67. B, The diskpart command has an option (clean all) to remove all contents from a connected drive.

68. D, The ipconfig command can display various amounts of information about the user's network connection, depending on which options are used.

69. C, You can use either the IP address or the URL with ping. However, the syntax must be correct.

70. D, The command *cd foldername* drops the focus of the command prompt down one level, and Miranda is in the next level below the Users folder

71. A, B. These two commands can be run from a command prompt to execute or kill a task.

72. D, The Event Viewer cannot anticipate events that may occur.

73. A, The User Configuration section over which the Computer Configuration section takes precedence.

74. A, The Device Manager should be used to investigate device issues.

75. B, The Registry key for the configuration and settings for the current user is HKEY_CURRENT_USER.

76. D, Internet Options is used to configure the Internet security zone.

77. C, The Network and Sharing Center is used to access the media streaming settings.

78. A, The Devices and Printers option is used for centralized viewing and management of monitors, printers, and peripheral devices.

79. B, The Control Panel provides tools and services to access and control the system settings and features.

80. D, From the Category view of the Control Panel, power settings are accessed through the System and Security category.

81. D, Windows will make suggestions or provide hints, but it doesn't make judgments.

82. B, The background tint is not a setting of the Display settings.

83. C, The settings for these devices are on the System section of the Settings app.

84. A, The Diagnostics & Feedback settings are in the Privacy section of the Settings app.

85. D, The settings for the Windows Lock screen are found on the Personalization section of the Settings app.

86. C, With the IP address of the printer, the user can find and set up the printer using Devices and Printers.

87. B, When Windows Firewall is set to Public, connections to LAN devices are blocked for security.

88. D, On most SOHO networks, the DHCP server that provides automatic IP addresses is a function built into the router. Thus, the router is the first device to check.

89. C, The network firewall rules may be denying the source IP address, the document type, or some other characteristic of the missing document.

90. A, It appears that an APIPA address was assigned automatically when a DHCP request failed.

91. D, A 32-bit app will work on 32-bit and 64-bit operating systems, but you cannot install a 64-bit app on a 32-bit operating system.

92. B, If you wait to install the app until you go to the airport or while onboard the plane, you might not have access to an Internet connection or might need to pay a lot for a connection (which might be very slow) to download and configure the software.

93. C, By upgrading some systems to 8 GB and running the app on all systems, you can determine if the performance difference between systems with 4 GB and 8 GB of RAM justifies upgrading all computers in the department.

94. C, The Compatibility tab in the application's Properties dialog box provides access to the Program Compatibility Troubleshooter and to compatibility settings you can select manually.

95. B, While all of the methods listed have one or more faults, using an external hardware token may be the easiest method for employees to work with, although there is still the issue of the token being lost.

96. B, A business operating system is better suited for the needs of workstations on larger networks.

97. A, Any of the choices could be the answer, but if you are attempting to be compatible with other users or systems, your best bet is likely Windows.

98. C, macOS is based on the UNIX OS.

99. B, C, Android and iOS are the most popular OSs for mobile devices. Windows Mobile has been deprecated, and there isn't a Linux Mobile product.

100.   B, D, The two file systems most common on Linux OSs are ext3 and ext4.

101.   C, it's always a good practice to back up user files and settings before proceeding with an installation or upgrade of any kind.

102.   B, A network boot configuration requires, among other components, a PXE network adapter.

103.   A, An image is a copy of an existing installation saved as one file.

104. A, An MBR partition has tangible limits of 2.2 TB and not more than four partitions.

105. C, A logical partition is assigned a drive letter.

106. A, Spotlight is the macOS search and indexing tool.

107. B, Force Quit is used to stop unresponsive apps.

108. A, Time Machine is the backup app for macOS.

109. D, One of the tools available to create scripts in macOS is launchd.

110. C, Passwords and login credentials from websites, e-mail accounts, and applications are saved to Keychain Access.

111. C, Many Linux commands must be run as the root user (superuser) with sudo.

112. B, The ps command lists active processes and their PIDs.

113. B, The cron command is used to control the start of a script using the time of day, day of the week, and so on.

114. C, The df command displays the amount of free disk space in 1-K blocks available on a Linux system.

115. C, Samba is used to connect a Linux system with a Windows system for interactions.

116. B, A security guard is helpful in making an access control vestibule (or mantrap) more effective and to maintain the entry control roster.

117. D, A USB lock prevents unused USB ports from being "borrowed" for data theft.

118. A, Different types of badge readers use these technologies.

119. C, The cable lock connector was developed by Kensington, hence the name.

120. C, Mobile device management (MDM) is software used to manage and control mobile devices that connect to a network.

121. C, This is single-factor authentication because the user name and password together are considered to be a single knowledge factor.

122. A, WPA3 replaced PSK with SAE.

123. C, Kerberos is used to authenticate web requests over the Internet and Web.

124. B, This is multifactor authentication because the user name/password combo is one factor (knowledge) and the code is the second factor (possession).

125. A, C, AES encryption offers 128-, 192-, and 256-bit encryption and is by far the strongest wireless encryption standard.

126. D, A ransomware attack combines file encryption and a demand for payment of a ransom before the files will be decrypted.

127. C, Instructing users in how to avoid e-mail traps is an example of end-user education.

128. D, User training and education should be the first line of defense and first-level priority to protect an organization from malware and social engineering attacks.

129. B, One sign of the presence of a cryptominer is an increase in electrical power use.

130. D, All of these OSs, plus Linux and iOS, provide a recovery mode of one form or another

131. A, A distributed denial of service (DDoS) attack comes from multiple locations, seeking to overwhelm a network resource so it can't respond.

132. B, The use of a false sender on the e-mail makes this an example of spoofing.

133. A, Dumpster diving involves taking discarded information from any location, not just a dumpster.

134. C, A zero-day attack takes place before or immediately after the software vendor discovers or has been provided knowledge of a vulnerability. It's called zero-day because the vendor has had zero days to patch the vulnerability.

135. D, A dictionary attack uses a list of possible matches for passwords. Since many users who create their own passwords often recycle old passwords in whole or in part, a list of old passwords can be very useful in the hands of an attacker.

136. C, A Microsoft account, while not universal, can be used to log in to most Microsoft applications and services.

137. D, BitLocker is not installed with the Windows 10/11 Home editions. The user can upgrade to another Windows edition or purchase BitLocker directly from the Microsoft Store.

138. E, At the present time, Spoken Passwords aren't available as a sign-in option.

139. B, Single sign-on (SSO) authenticates a user over multiple applications.

140. A, This option sets the UAC to always display a notification for any changes, including trusted Windows settings.

141. B, The strongest passwords use a mixture of upper- and lowercase letters, numbers, and symbols without recognized words.

142.   A, Account Lockout Policy prevents login attempts after a specified number of incorrect logins.

143.   C, AutoPlay is the feature that opens an app or lists a choice of apps based on the contents of the removable media.

144.   A, The Enforce Password History value sets the number of password changes that must occur before a password can be reused.

145.   D, Data stored on any form of media is considered to be "at rest."

146.   A, C, Remote wipe could wipe out the device's contents after it was determined to be lost or stolen; device encryption (a manual process on many devices) could prevent the device's contents from being accessed.

147.   B, If the option to wipe data after ten unsuccessful logins has been enabled in Settings | Passcode, the user is very close to losing his data, which is hopefully backed up to iCloud.

148.   D, Who owns company data on a BYOD device is an important issue in a BYOD policy.

149.   A, Facial recognition locks compare a previously captured image to a realtime image.

150.   A, The operations and communications of an IoT device are controlled by embedded devices, which typically include a microprocessor, operating system, and a network adapter.

151.   A, Drilling through the memory chip(s) will render the contents unrecoverable.

152.   B, A certificate of destruction from a third-party data destruction facility is what you need; the facility will decide the best methods and tools to use.

153.   C, Drive wiping would be the biggest concern.

154.   C, Formatting doesn't remove or overwrite data, so it is no substitute for drive wiping.

155.   D, Degaussing is the only suitable method of those listed for destroying data on magnetic tape.

156.   A, B, D These settings are not only standard to the devices but are publicly shared by the manufacturers.

157.   A, Using a web browser is the standard method for configuring and managing a router's settings.

158.   A, Port forwarding/mapping enables you to open a port in the firewall and direct incoming traffic on that port to a specific IP address on your LAN.

159.   D, A screened subnet does not include the role of WAN router.

160. B, IP filtering blocks incoming or outgoing messages based on their source and destination addresses.

161. A, B, It's safe to assume that the software obtained from what is obviously an untrusted site contained malware.

162. C, An extension adds a function to a browser that is executed externally to the browser itself.

163. B, A plug-in executes within the browser as an additional feature.

164. C, A padlock symbol on the address bar indicates a site is trusted.

165. B, Synchronization establishes a link between devices and apps to keep data up to date on the synched devices.

166. B, You must use the BIOS/UEFI firmware dialog box to change the boot order.

167. C, Rolling back the device driver will not affect other parts of the system, so it is the preferred method.

168. D, USB drives that are plugged in could prevent the system from restarting.

169. A, The other items listed are likely causes; the number of tasks running has a small impact on load time, but not as much impact as the others.

170. D, Safe Mode Repair is not a WinRE troubleshooting advanced option.

171. A, Malware has caused the user to open a page without a trusted certificate.

172. C, An APIPA address cannot be used beyond a local network.

173. B, A false alert occurs when malware erroneously identifies valid data or files as bad.

174. C, A warning message seeks confirmation that the user wishes to proceed.

175. B, Pop-ups are typically displayed by malware that has infected a web page.

176. B, Software can be damaged by malware, so repairing it may be a part of remediation on some systems.

177. D, Clean booting or booting from a USB or optical disc before running malware removal helps prevent malware from running and interfering with the removal process.

178. C, The restore point needs to remember the system configuration after it has been remediated and protected against threats.

179. D, Determining that a malware infection is present is included in Step 1: Investigate and verify malware symptoms.

180. A, B, Boot into the Windows Preinstallation Environment (WinPE) and use the Windows Recovery Environment (WinRE) tools to recover the system.

181. B, The performance of a mobile device may be improved by a system reset.

182. C, A force stop stops an app and any supporting services.

183. A, B, C, Any or all of these conditions could be the issue.

184. B, But more may be better in certain instances.

185. C, Most likely the Airplane mode is still enabled.

186. B, Malware can use a lot of resources because it captures and sends data without the user's permission or knowledge.

187. B, Sideloading occurs when a system file is loaded from an untrusted site.

188. D, Developer mode opens several apps and files not usually available to a standard user.

189. A, B, These tools can be used to detect and profile the actions of a malware infection.

190. B, Rooting can void a device's warranty.

191. A, A network topology diagram must record the network's physical layout. The other items are desirable to know but not essential.

192. C, A third-party system information app can provide much more information than the System Properties dialog box in Windows.

193. B, Keyboard lighting is a feature found mainly on gaming keyboards and some laptops and won't affect typical operations covered in an AUP.

194. D, The asset must be identified with a unique asset identification number.

195. B, C, The network diagram and the installed equipment information are considered key operational knowledge.

196. C, A rollback (backout) plan is designed to help an organization return to pre-change conditions if a change has an adverse impact.

197. D, Risk analysis is a necessary part of change management. The other choices, not so much.

198. A, Without documenting changes, the knowledge of what has changed will fade over time

199. C, End users and other stakeholders must have the opportunity to review proposed changes and how they may affect their tasks.

200. D, A responsible staff member should be appointed to oversee the implementation.

Walking into the exam center, your heartbeat might be a tad faster, and your palms slightly sweaty; it's a common experience, but this chapter aims to give you the composure and focus you need to excel. We've covered an extensive amount of material, from network topologies to disaster recovery, but this chapter focuses solely on the practical aspects of the day that will decide your certification fate.

The first order of business is to have a clear understanding of the exam location and logistics. While this may seem rudimentary, you would be surprised how many candidates misjudge travel time or get lost on the way to the testing center. A prior visit to the center a few days before the exam can significantly reduce any unexpected hiccups. Get to know the area, the traffic conditions, and even the parking availability. On the day of the exam, aim to arrive at least 30 minutes early. This gives you enough time to adjust to the environment, complete necessary check-ins, and even review some last-minute notes.

When it comes to your mental state, a well-rested mind is crucial for peak performance. Lack of sleep can impact your cognitive functions, reduce your focus, and make you prone to mistakes. Therefore, try to get a good night's sleep before the exam day and resist the urge to do any last-minute cramming. Relax, unwind, and trust the preparation you've put in. Confidence, not overconfidence, is key.

As for what to bring to the exam, most centers will require two forms of identification. Usually, one of them has to be a government-issued ID with a photograph. Read through all the exam guidelines beforehand to ensure you are not missing any essentials. You'll also be provided a small locker to store personal items, as you usually can't bring anything into the exam room itself. Ensure your mobile phones are turned off and stored securely to avoid any disruptions.

You can expect the CompTIA Network+ exam to include multiple-choice questions, drag-and-drop activities, and performance-based questions. Time management is paramount. While it's easy to get stuck on a complex question, it's essential to move on if it's taking too much time. Flag the question for review and return to it after completing the rest of the exam. Remember, not answering a question guarantees zero points, so it's better to take an educated guess if you're uncertain.

When seated at the exam terminal, take a few deep breaths to center yourself. This is the moment where you need to draw upon all the knowledge and skills you've developed. Remember, you've prepared extensively for this. Your readiness isn't just a result of the weeks or months leading up to this day but is the culmination of your educational and professional journey to date.

Lastly, after completing the exam, you will be prompted to review your flagged questions. Use this opportunity wisely but also know that second-guessing yourself can be counterproductive. If you studied well and followed this guide, your first instinct is usually the correct one.

After submitting the exam, you'll receive a preliminary score immediately, and while the wait for the official results can be nerve-wracking, take this time to unwind and decompress. Whether you pass or need to retake the exam, remember that this is a learning experience, and each attempt brings you closer to becoming a certified Network+ professional.

In conclusion, the day of your CompTIA Network+ exam will likely be filled with a blend of anxiety and excitement. However, your diligent preparation combined with these exam day tips can make the difference between certification and having to retake the exam. Good luck, and may your knowledge and skills carry you through to a successful and rewarding career in networking.

Conclusion

As we close the final chapter of this comprehensive guide aimed at propelling you toward success in the CompTIA Network+ exam, it's important to reflect on the transformative journey we've embarked upon together. Through various sections, we've dissected the realms of networking, from its most basic building blocks to the complex fabric that holds modern enterprises together. But acquiring this knowledge is not an endpoint; rather, it's the genesis of a career-long journey in the ever-evolving field of networking.

Achieving the CompTIA Network+ certification isn't merely a validation of your skills for the current job market; it's an investment in your professional future. The networking landscape is continually reshaped by emerging technologies and evolving security threats, and this certification equips you with the foundational knowledge you need to adapt and grow. It opens doors for further specialization, whether in security, cloud computing, or network design, and serves as a launchpad for vendor-specific certifications that can further elevate your career.

Speaking of career trajectories, let's not overlook the vital aspect of continual learning. The field of networking is not static. The pace at which new technologies, standards, and protocols are introduced necessitates an attitude of perpetual learning. Subscriptions to industry journals, participation in online forums, and ongoing training are not luxuries; they are necessities for staying relevant. Therefore, consider this book not as an ending but as a stepping stone to more advanced topics and deeper understanding.

Exam day will soon arrive, and when it does, remember that your best ally is your state of mind. Stress and anxiety are natural but counterproductive. You've prepared rigorously and are well-equipped to face the challenges of the CompTIA Network+ exam. Confidence, born from your meticulous preparation, will be your strongest asset. Go through the questions methodically, utilize your time wisely, and rely on your acquired knowledge and skills.

One often overlooked aspect of career development is networking—not in the technical sense, but in the interpersonal one. No matter how advanced or secure a network is, it is ultimately designed, maintained, and managed by people. Attending industry conferences, engaging with mentors, and even participating in online networking groups can provide invaluable opportunities for career growth. A well-placed recommendation can sometimes be more effective than a well-configured router in advancing your career.

Finally, let's consider the essence of what it means to be a Network+ certified professional. You're not just a technician or an administrator; you're a problem solver, a gatekeeper of information, and a facilitator of communication. You have the responsibility to uphold the integrity, availability, and confidentiality of your organization's network. It's a significant role that has ripple effects across all departments of an organization, and now, you are fully prepared to take on that role.

In conclusion, while this guide has provided you with the tools and knowledge to pass the CompTIA Network+ exam, the ultimate key to success lies within you: your dedication, your curiosity, and your relentless pursuit of excellence. Certification is a milestone, not a destination. Welcome to the dynamic, challenging, and rewarding world of networking.